The Complete Photo Guide to

COOKIE DECORATING

Creative Publishing international

First published in the United States of America by Creative Publishing international, Inc., a member of Quayside Publishing Group
400 First Avenue North
Suite 300
Minneapolis, MN 55401
1-800-328-3895
www.creativepub.com

ISBN: 978-1-58923-748-3

Printed in China

10 9 8 7 6 5 4 3 2 1

Library of Congress Cataloging-in-Publication Data available

Copy Editor: Catherine Broberg
Proofreader: Karen Ruth
Book and Cover Design: Kim Winscher
Page Layout: Laurie Young
Photographs: Dan Brand and Autumn Carpenter

The Complete Photo Guide to
COOKIE DECORATING

Creative Publishing
international

CONTENTS

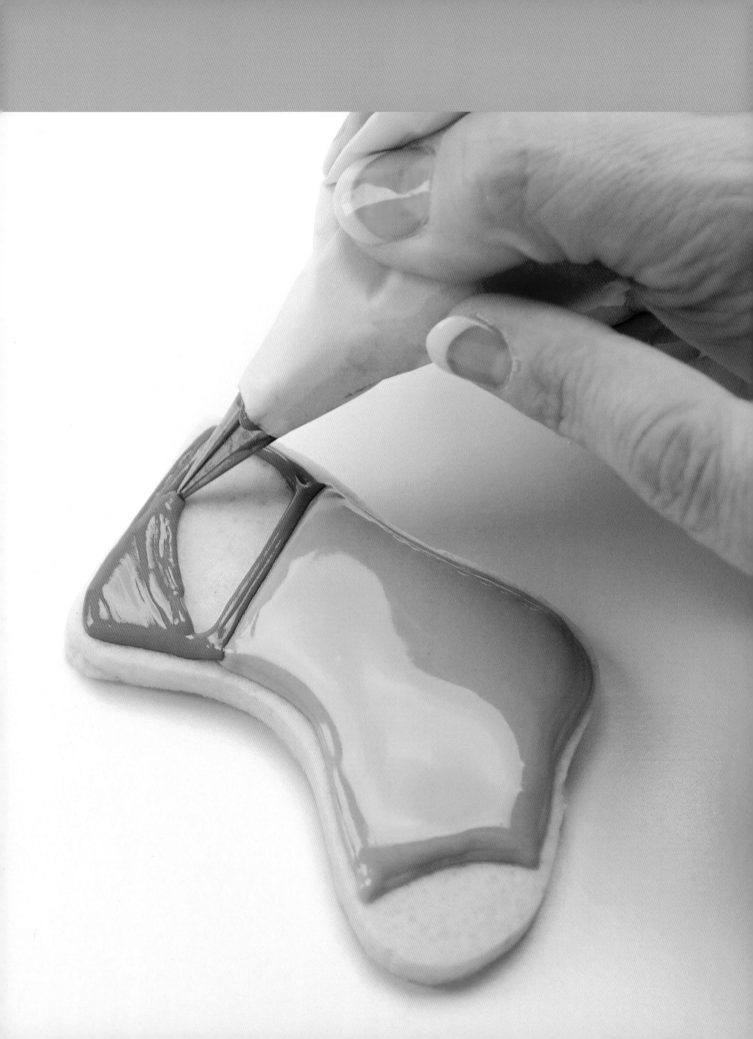

Introduction

Cookie decorating has become a popular art in the confectionary field. Crafters and bakers alike find cookie decorating extremely gratifying. In just a few minutes, a cookie can be transformed from a simple shape into a colorful, edible work of art. Today cookies are not just decorated for the holidays. Cookies are often a dessert for a party, given as party favors, or made for gift-giving on special occasions.

This book is a comprehensive guide to the vast world of cookie decorating. If you are new to cookie decorating, use the book to choose techniques that look intriguing. If you have decorated cookies before, use this book to brush up on what you've already learned and pick up some great new tips.

This book features several icings and techniques and explores each of them deeply. Along with the easy-to-follow, step-by-step instructions on using these icings, there are photo galleries with dozens of popular themes to inspire your cookie decorating.

Before jumping right into decorating cookies, take time to read Baking Cookies for basic cutout recipes. After all, a good cookie is the foundation of cookie decorating—and will taste delicious with or without icing. Follow the simple instructions and tips on rolling or molding cookie dough to ensure your cookies are perfectly baked every time. Learn how to bake cookies with a stick for cookie arrangements.

Cookie Icings begins with the tools and edible decorations needed to decorate cookies. The chapters following cover several icings, each offering unique qualities. Within each chapter you'll discover step-by-step instructions and pictures to help you master the decorating techniques. The most classic cookie icing is run sugar. Along with the basics of run sugar, learn how to create run sugar marble patterns in contrasting colors as well as painting on run sugar. If your cookies are not picture-perfect, the troubleshooting section will pinpoint what went wrong. Rolled fondant is a cookie covering like no other. The claylike material is rolled and can be textured to produce a decorated cookie.

Buttercream is a super sweet icing that is spread or piped onto the cookie for various textures and dimension. The egg wash glaze provides a light coating with a subtle sheen to molded cookies. Candy coating is another icing included for a delicious coated cookie. Instructions include using chocolate transfer sheets to achieve fun patterns on candy-coated cookies.

Miscellaneous Techniques offers tips to help you further enhance your cookie decorating skills. Learn how to create cookies with shimmer and sparkle using sugars, edible sprays, and dusting powders. Other unique techniques include flocking, eyelet, brush embroidery, rolled fondant accents, stencils, and edible frosting sheets. Learn how to assemble a cookie bouquet. Be inspired with the packaging ideas.

For those who might be a bit intimidated by the idea of decorating cookies, fear not! It is not as hard as you might think. Most decorating techniques require trial and error to achieve a flawless decorated cookie, but cookie decorating is an art. And everyone from children to adults can create this edible art.

My hope is that, whether you're a beginner or advanced decorator, you will find as much enjoyment from all these fantastic techniques as I do and use the book to be inspired to create your own cookie designs.

Autumn

BAKING COOKIES

A perfectly baked cookie provides the base to a beautifully decorated cookie. The tips and instructions in this section will help ensure your cookies are even in thickness, baked just right, and taste great. All of the cookies featured in the book were baked using the baking tools, dough recipes, and baking instructions included in this section. Learn how to create perfect cut-out cookies with a smooth work surface for the icing, how to bake a cookie on a stick for cookie arrangements, and how to mold and stamp cookie dough. The cookie dough recipes yield cookies with a simple, subtle sweetness. The icing recipes in the second section complement any of the cookie recipes.

Tools for Baking

The following tools are useful for baking cookies. Necessities include a rolling pin, cookie sheet, cooling rack, and cutters or molds. Other tools, such as perfection strips and flour shakers, are not essential but make the rolling and cutting process more efficient.

COOKIE SHEETS

Cookie sheets come in a variety of finishes, styles, and sizes. Choose a shiny silver, generously sized cookie sheet with no sides or one side. Be sure the cookie sheet you choose is not too big for your oven; there should be at least 1" (2.5 cm) between the oven wall and cookie sheet for even heat circulation. A 14" x 20" (35.6 x 50.8 cm) cookie sheet is generous in size and fits in standard ovens, while allowing enough air circulation. A cookie sheet with no sides or one side allows a cookie spatula to be easily slid under the cookie near the edges of the sheet. Cookie sheets with a dark finish tend to brown the bottoms of the cookies too quickly. Do not grease cookie sheets unless the recipe calls for grease. Too much grease may cause cookie dough to spread. Use parchment paper or silicone baking mats to keep cookies from sticking to the cookie sheet. Keep two or three cookies sheets on hand for efficient cookie baking. Allow cookie sheets to cool between batches; placing cookie dough on hot cookie sheets will cause the cookies to spread.

ROLLING PINS

The two most popular styles of rolling pins for rolling cookie dough are classic rolling pins with handles or baker's rolling pins (rolling pins without handles). Rolling pins with handles should have ball bearings for ease in rolling. I prefer a baker's rolling pin because the weight is distributed on the barrel rather than the handles, which may cause fatigue in the hands and wrist. Be aware that it takes a bit of practice to master rolling the cookie dough using a rolling pin without handles.

Choose a rolling pin that is wide enough to handle a large sheet of cookie dough. The more the cookie dough is rolled, the more the dough becomes over-worked. Rolling pins with a short barrel may be easier to handle, but the dough will need to be re-rolled several more times compared to a rolling pin with a longer barrel.

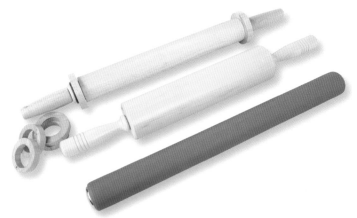

Rolling pins are made of various materials. Wood and silicone are the most popular. Silicone rolling pins are ideal for rolling cookie dough because of the stick-resistant surface. Wooden rolling pins are available in a variety of sizes.

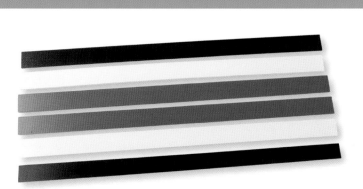

Some rolling pins come with rings. The rings fit on each end of the barrel to allow the dough to be rolled evenly. Rings may also be purchased separately. These rings may only fit on a barrel with specific diameters. Perfection strips (see above) are an alternative to rolling pin rings.

PERFECTION STRIPS

For successful cutouts, the dough must be rolled perfectly even. Perfection strips come in a set with several different thicknesses. Place the cookie dough in between two strips of the same size. Roll over the strips and the dough will be a consistent thickness. A rolling pin with rings can be used instead of perfection strips (see above).

FLOUR SHAKER

Flour shakers allow an excellent amount of control when dispersing flour onto the work surface or cookie dough.

SILICONE BAKING MATS AND PARCHMENT PAPER

To keep cookies from becoming too tough, eliminate flour when rolling cookie dough. Parchment paper provides a nonstick surface when rolling dough. A silicone mat may also be used when rolling cookie dough; however, the mat may need a dusting of flour to prevent the dough from sticking.

Silicone baking mats and parchment paper may also be used when baking cookies. Baked cookies will not stick to cookie sheets lined with parchment paper or a silicone

mat. It is handy to have two or three silicone baking mats on hand to keep the baking process efficient. Silicone mats and parchment paper cool quickly after being removed from a hot cookie sheet. After the parchment paper or mat cools completely, reuse by rolling out more dough or baking more cookies on it.

To bake cookies on the same parchment paper or silicone mat the dough was rolled on, simply remove excess dough after cutting out shapes but leave the cut cookies in place. Slide the baking mat or parchment paper with the cutout cookies onto a cookie sheet, and bake.

Silicone baking mats come in several sizes. Measure your cookie sheet and select a mat the same size or slightly smaller than the cookie sheet. Parchment paper comes on a roll or in precut sheets. Parchment paper can be reused a few times during the same baking day.

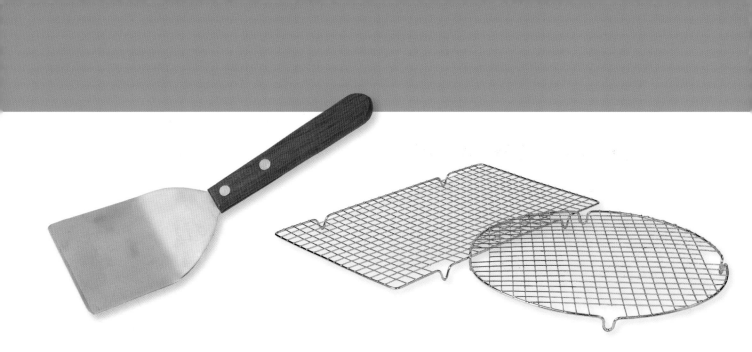

COOKIE SPATULA

A cookie spatula is a spatula with a wide, thin blade. Use a cookie spatula to easily transfer cutout unbaked cookies from the work surface to the cookie sheet. The spatula is also handy for moving baked cookies from the cookie sheets to cooling racks. When transferring cookies from cookie sheets to cooling racks, the cookies will still be soft. Using a cookie spatula with a wide blade prevents the cookies from breaking at this stage.

COOKIE CUTTERS

Thousands of cookie-cutter shapes are available in nearly every theme imaginable and in a variety of finishes. The most popular finishes are copper, tinplate, plastic, plastic-coated metal, and stainless steel. I typically do not choose cookie cutters based on type of finish, but rather by the size and shape. Tinplate cutters tend to be a favorite because they are inexpensive. Tinplate will bend easier than copper or stainless steel, but in most cases can be bent back to the original shape. Because tinplate is more flexible, cutters can be distorted, if desired, to create a specific shape. For example, a round cutter can be formed into an Easter egg shape. On the other hand, copper and stainless steel are more durable and will hold their shape after cutting dozens of cookies. Copper cutters most often are not as sharp as tinplate cutters. Care must be given when cleaning all metal cutters as they may rust or discolor if not thoroughly dried after washing. Plastic cutters or plastic-coated metal cutters do not rust.

COOLING RACK

It is important to cool cookies on a cooling rack so air circulates on all sides of the cookies. Cookies that are left to cool on the counter may become soggy on the bottom. Choose a cooling rack with closely arranged wires in a grid pattern to prevent smaller cookies from slipping. Stacking cooling racks are convenient when space is an issue.

Also, they are often not as sharp as other cookie cutters, making them an obvious choice when making cookies with children. If the shape desired is unavailable, there are even cookie cutter kits to create your own designs.

PARING KNIVES

A paring knife is a must-have for removing excess cookie dough from cookies spaced tightly together or cookies with intricate details.

COOKIE MOLDS AND STAMPS

Elegantly detailed cookies may be created without any icing or decorating, using cookie molds or cookie stamps. Hand-carved wooden cookie molds and wooden cookie mold replicas can be quite costly, but provide intricate detail. Inexpensive hard-candy molds may also be used to bake cookies. Molds should have consistent thickness.

Cookie stamps are used to press a ball of cookie dough into a circle with embossed details. Whether using a cookie mold or stamp, use a cookie dough that holds its shape when baked. All of the recipes included in this book are suitable for molding and stamping.

Cookie Recipes

The recipes in this book all create firm cookies with a perfect surface for cookie icings. Each recipe yields cookies with a simple, subtle sweetness that is enhanced with icing. All of the cookie recipes in this chapter will hold their shape when baked.

If using a recipe not included in this book, eliminate any leavening agents to prevent the cookies from spreading. Baked cookies, with or without icing, taste best when eaten within seven to ten days. When mixing the dough, a stand mixer with a flat beater attachment is ideal, but a hand mixer may be used. The cookie dough recipes have different working properties. Some cookie dough requires chilling in the refrigerator before rolling or molding, while others are ready to use immediately. If the dough needs to be chilled, flatten the dough into a patty approximately 1½" (3.8 cm) thick to expedite the chilling time. Wrap tightly with plastic wrap and refrigerate. Each

recipe includes a yield for 3" to 4" (7.6 to 10.2 cm) cookies. The yield varies with the cookie thickness and size of cutters.

BUTTERY SUGAR COOKIES

After trying dozens of sugar cookie recipes over the years, I always come back to this recipe. It is simple to mix, and it rolls and freezes beautifully. It is important to chill the dough to firm the cream cheese and butter. If this dough is rolled immediately after mixing, additional flour may be needed when rolling, which will toughen the dough. The flavor can be altered by replacing vanilla with other extracts. Some of my favorite replacements are orange and lemon. If I replace the vanilla with a different extract, I will often add the same extract in my icing to add additional flavor.

Important Recipe Tips

- Always use high-quality ingredients. Butter is superior to margarine. While low-fat ingredients may produce cookies that are better for you, the taste and baking properties will be compromised. Allow refrigerated ingredients such as butter or cream cheese 30 minutes to 1 hour to come to room temperature before mixing.

- Be sure to properly measure when mixing dough. Not enough flour can make the dough difficult and sticky to roll; too much flour will cause the cookie to be tough and dry. When measuring flour, scoop the flour into the measuring cup so that flour is overflowing. Use the straight edge of a knife or spatula to scrape the excess flour.

- If a baked cookie breaks, repair it with royal icing. When decorating, the icing will cover up the crack.

Buttery Sugar Cookie Recipe

- *1 cup (2 sticks [225 gl] of unsalted butter, softened*
- *3 ounces (85 g) cream cheese, softened*
- *¾ cup (170 g) sugar*
- *1 egg*
- *1 teaspoon (5 mL) vanilla*
- *3 cups (330 g) all-purpose flour*

1 Mix the butter and cream cheese with an electric mixer on medium speed for 2 or 3 minutes or until the butter and cream cheese are blended. Scrape the bowl.

2 Add the sugar. Continue to blend on medium speed until the mixture is light and fluffy. Mix in the vanilla.

3 Add the egg, mixing on low until thoroughly blended. Scrape the bowl.

4 Add the flour, 1 cup (110 g) at a time. Scrape the bowl after adding each cup. Mix until just incorporated. Do not overmix, or the dough will toughen.

5 Divide the dough into two equal portions. Flatten the dough into 2 patties that are approximately 1½" (3.8 cm) thick. Wrap the patties with plastic wrap and refrigerate at least 2 hours, or until firm.

6 Roll out and cut the cookies (page 18). Bake the cookies in a 375°F (190°C) oven. Bake for 9 to 11 minutes or until edges are very lightly browned.

Yields 36 (3" to 4" [7.6 to 10.2 cm] cookies)

CHOCOLATE COOKIES FOR CUTOUTS

These delicious chocolate sugar cookies have a flavor similar to a brownie. The type of cocoa powder used will change the flavor and color of the cookie. Dutch cocoa powders tend to have a richer color and flavor. Replace the vanilla flavor with peppermint or mocha extract for a fun twist on a classic chocolate cookie. After mixing the dough, it is ready to use immediately. This cookie dough tends to be a bit more crumbly when rolling, and the cookies can easily be overcooked. It is difficult to know when these cookies are done baking as the edges do not brown. If they are overbaked, they become very crisp.

Chocolate Sugar Cookie Recipe

- *1 cup (225 g) butter, softened*
- *1½ cup (340 g) sugar*
- *2 eggs*
- *2 teaspoons (10 mL) vanilla*
- *3 cups (330 g) all-purpose flour*
- *⅔ cup (75 g) unsweetened cocoa powder*
- *½ teaspoon (2.5 mL) salt*

1 In a large bowl, blend the flour, cocoa powder, and salt.

2 Mix the butter and sugar with an electric mixer on medium speed for 2 or 3 minutes or until the mixture is light and fluffy. Scrape the bowl.

3 Add the eggs and vanilla and mix on low until thoroughly blended. Scrape the bowl.

4 Add the flour mixture, 1 cup (110 g) at a time. Scrape the bowl after adding each cup of flour. Mix until just incorporated. Do not overmix, or the dough will toughen.

5 Divide the dough into two equal portions. Flatten the dough into two patties that are approximately 1½" (3.8 cm) thick. Use the dough immediately, or refrigerate until ready to mold or roll.

6 Bake the cookies in a 350°F (175°C) oven. Bake for 8 to 10 minutes or until no indentation is made when touched.

Yields 36 (3" to 4" [7.6 to 10.2 cm] cookies)

Cracking or Sticking

If the dough cracks or breaks when rolling, it is likely too cold to roll. Allow the dough to come to room temperature. If the dough is sticking, it did not chill long enough or it has gotten warm as it has been rolled. Too much cream cheese or butter may also cause sticking. Place the dough in the refrigerator for 1 or 2 hours. If the dough is still sticking, dust the work surface and the top of the cookie dough with a bit of flour.

GINGERBREAD COOKIES

These gingerbread cookies are a crisp cookie. The recipe holds up well for projects using gingerbread. The dough should be used immediately. Baked cookies become distorted if the dough is not used within a few hours. Overworking the dough may also create distorted cookies. Roll the dough only a couple times.

Gingerbread Cookie Recipe

- ¼ cup (55 g) butter, softened
- ½ cup (100 g) brown sugar
- ½ cup (120 mL) molasses
- 3 cups (330 g) flour, sifted
- 1 teaspoon (5 mL) cinnamon
- 1 teaspoon (5 mL) ginger
- ¼ teaspoon (1.5 mL) nutmeg
- ⅓ cup (80 mL) water

1 In a large bowl, blend 1 cup (110 g) of the flour with the cinnamon, ginger, and nutmeg.

2 On medium speed, beat butter and brown sugar together until creamy, 2 or 3 minutes, or until the mixture is light and fluffy. Scrape the bowl. Beat in the molasses.

3 Mix in the flour and spice mixture. Add the remaining 2 cups (220 g) of flour alternately with ⅓ cup (80 mL) water. It may be necessary to knead the last cup of flour by hand if the dough feels stiff. Scrape the bowl after adding each cup of flour. Mix until just incorporated. Do not overmix, or the dough will toughen.

4 Bake the cookies in a 350°F (175°C) oven. Bake for 8 to 10 minutes or until no indentation is made when touched.

Yields 40 (3" to 4" [7.6 to 10.2 cm] cookies)

PERFECTION SPRINGERLE COOKIES

Springerle cookies are whisked-egg cookies that date back to at least the 1600s. The dense cake-like cookies mold beautifully. Traditional Springerle cookies are molded with wooden molds containing deep carvings. Although these cookies may be made with baking powder, baker's ammonia provides a softer cookie. Anise flavor is the conventional flavor used for Springerle cookies, but other flavors may be used. Connie Meisinger, a talented cookie artist, provides the recipes and instructions included in this chapter. Connie's company, House on the Hill (www.houseonthehill.net) offers dozens of intricate wooden molds for sale as well as tips and recipes.

Springerle Cookie Recipe

- ½ teaspoon (2.5 mL) baker's ammonia (hartshorn) or baking powder
- 2 tablespoons (30 mL) milk
- 6 large eggs, room temperature
- 6 cups powdered sugar (1½ lb [0.68 kg])
- ½ cup (115 g) unsalted butter, softened but not melted
- ½ teaspoon (2.5 mL) salt
- ½ teaspoon (2.5 mL) anise (if substituting fruit-flavored oils, use 3 teaspoons [15 mL])
- 2-pound (0.91 kg) box sifted cake flour (Swansdown or Softasilk)
- grated rind of orange or lemon, optional (enhances flavor of the traditional anise or the citrus flavors)
- more flour as needed

1 Dissolve the baker's ammonia in milk and set aside. Beat eggs until thick and lemon colored (10 to 20 minutes). Slowly beat in the powdered sugar, then the softened butter. Add the baker's ammonia and milk mixture, salt, anise or preferred flavoring, and grated lemon or orange rind. Gradually beat in as much of the flour as you can with the mixer; then stir in the remainder of the 2 pounds (0.91 kg) of flour to make a stiff dough.

2 Turn the dough onto a floured surface and knead in enough flour to make a good print without sticking.

3 Roll the dough approximately ⅜" (1 cm) thick (deeper molds require thicker dough). Brush confectioner's sugar or flour on the mold image; then imprint with a wooden mold. Trim around the shape using a knife, cookie cutter, or pastry wheel. Imprint one design; then trim around the imprinted cookie. Do not imprint all designs at once, and then cut, or the adjacent images may become distorted. Allow the printed cookie to dry for 2 to 24 hours before baking (depending on your schedule, humidity, etc.). Drying preserves the image during baking.

4 Bake on greased or parchment-lined cookie sheets at 255°F to 325°F (125°C to 160°C) until barely golden on the bottom, 10–15 minutes or more, depending on size of cookie. Store in airtight containers or in zipper bags in the freezer. They keep for months and improve with age.

Yields 36 (3" to 4" [7.6 to 10.2 cm] cookies)

STORING COOKIE DOUGH

Cookie dough can be stored in the refrigerator up to a week. After mixing the cookie dough, flatten it into a large circular patty about 1½" (3.8 cm) thick. Tightly wrap with plastic wrap and place in the refrigerator. Allow the dough to warm to nearly room temperature before rolling or molding. All of the cookie dough recipes in this book freeze well. The dough can be kept for up to three months in the freezer. To freeze, wrap the cookie dough with two or three layers of plastic wrap. Wrap again with a layer of foil. When ready to thaw, place the frozen dough in the refrigerator for several hours.

Allow the dough to warm to nearly room temperature before rolling or molding.

SHELF LIFE OF BAKED COOKIES

Generally, cutout cookies have a longer shelf life than most baked goods. I prefer to have my cookies eaten within seven to ten days, but most cutout cookies will keep up to three weeks. The icing recipes included in this book will keep for several weeks at room temperature. It is the baked cookie, not the icing, that determines the shelf life. Refrigerating the decorated cookie may cause the icing colors to bleed or develop spots. For best results, store decorated cookies according to the specific instructions for each icing recipe.

FREEZING BAKED COOKIES

Cookies that are cut out and baked freeze beautifully. Decorated cookies, on the other hand, do not freeze well. Colors bleed or spotting occurs. The icing used will determine if the decorated cookie is suited to freeze. Refer to the storage information for the particular icing when deciding whether to freeze decorated cookies.

To freeze undecorated cookies, allow the baked cookies to completely cool. Place the cookies in a single layer in a box. Place a sheet of parchment paper on top of the first layer. Add additional cookies in single layers until reaching the top edge of the box. Close the box. Tightly wrap the box with two or three layers of plastic wrap; then wrap with a layer of foil. Place the sealed box in the freezer. Remove the box from the freezer several hours before you plan to decorate the cookies. Place the box of frozen cookies on the counter. Do not remove the plastic wrap or foil until the cookies have come to room temperature. Once the cookies have thawed and are at room temperature, they are ready to decorate.

Rolling Cookie Dough and Cutting Shapes

To achieve a cookie with perfect thickness, use perfection strips. Or use a rolling pin with rings. Some rolling pins include rings or rings are available separately. If you need to buy the rings, measure the rolling pin barrel; its diameter determines which rings will be appropriate. The rolling-pin diameter varies with the brand. Your choice of icing determines which size of perfection strips or rolling pin rings to use. Cookies with a thick layer of a sweet icing, such as piped buttercream, should have a baked cookie with a thickness of at least ¼" (6 mm). If the cookie is thin and the buttercream is piled high, the icing will overpower the cookie. Cookies with a thin layer of icing, such as run sugar, can be rolled thinner to approximately ⅛" (4 mm).

Roll the cookie dough and then cut shapes using one of the two methods shown. For best results, the dough should be cool but not so cold that it is difficult to roll. Removing the dough from the refrigerator an hour before rolling will usually be enough time for the dough to warm to a good temperature for rolling.

In the first method, the cookie dough is rolled on a silicone baking mat or sheet of parchment. After the dough is rolled, the shapes are cut and the excess dough is removed, leaving the cut shape untouched. The silicone mat or parchment sheet is then slid onto a cookie sheet and the cookies are baked. The advantage of this method is that you will have perfectly shaped cookies with no distortion. This is especially important when letter or geometric shapes are cut. Avoiding distortion is also important if the cookie is to be covered in rolled fondant, because the same cutter that was used in baking the cookie is also used to cut the rolled fondant. The disadvantage of this method is that it creates more excess dough that will need to be rerolled, and this overworks the cookie dough. Another disadvantage is that you may not be able to bake as many cookies at a time.

In the second method of rolling and cutting, the chilled cookie dough is placed on a nonstick work surface such as parchment paper or a silicone baking mat that has been lightly dusted with flour. Once the cookie dough is rolled, the shapes are cut and transferred to a cookie sheet lined with parchment paper or a silicone mat and the cookies are ready to bake. The advantage of this method is that more cookies can be baked at a time and the dough is less likely to become overworked. The disadvantage is that the cookies may become distorted if care is not taken when transferring the cut shape to the cookie sheet. Another disadvantage is that the rolling surface is dusted with flour and that will be absorbed by the cookie dough, which may cause the baked cookies to be tough. When dusting the work surface with flour, use a small amount. If the dough is still sticking when rolled, place the dough in the refrigerator to chill.

ROLLING THE DOUGH AND TRANSFERRING THE PARCHMENT PAPER TO A COOKIE SHEET

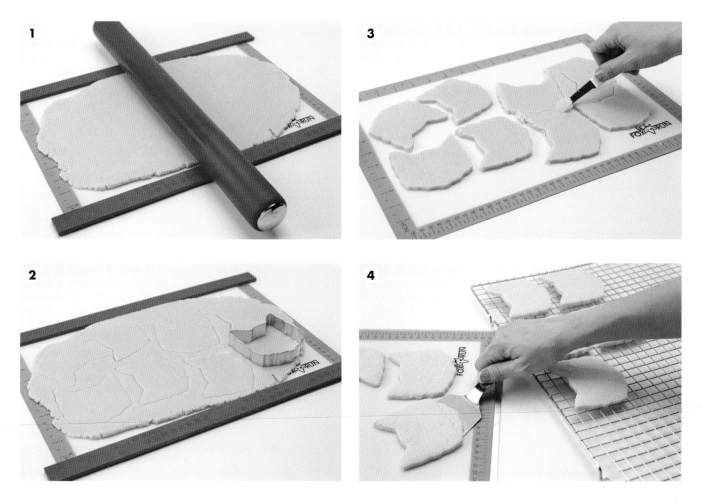

1 Start with chilled dough. Place the cookie dough between perfection strips on a silicone mat or a sheet of parchment paper. Roll over the strips, leveling the cookie dough.

2 Use a cookie cutter to cut shapes approximately ¼" (6 mm) apart. The cookies in this book hold their shape so they can be cut very close together, eliminating excessive working of the dough.

3 Remove the excess dough using a paring knife. The scraps can be rerolled and more shapes can be cut.

4 Slide the parchment paper or silicone mat onto a cookie sheet. Bake the cookies according to the recipe instructions. After the cookies are baked, allow them to cool for 3 to 4 minutes on the cookie sheet. Use a cookie spatula to gently transfer the warm, cut shapes to a cooling rack. Baked cookies will be fragile and soft to touch while they are still hot. Take extra care when moving the baked cookie from the cookie sheet to the cooling rack. Allow the cookies to cool completely before decorating.

ROLLING THE DOUGH AND TRANSFERRING THE CUT SHAPE TO A COOKIE SHEET

1 Start with chilled dough. Place the cookie dough between perfection strips on a sheet of parchment paper. Roll over the strips, leveling the cookie dough. A silicone baking mat may also be used to roll the dough, but the dough tends to stick more to silicone than parchment paper. The dough may also be rolled on a countertop dusted with flour. Use as little flour as possible to avoid toughening the dough. If the dough is sticking to the parchment paper or silicone mat, it will be difficult to remove the cut cookie shapes. The parchment paper or silicone mat can be lightly dusted with flour if the cookie dough is sticking.

2 Line a cookie sheet with a sheet of parchment paper or a silicone mat. Use a cookie cutter to cut shapes. Cut the shapes as close together as possible. Ideally, the dough will remain in the cookie cutter after the shape is cut. This will eliminate any distortion. If the dough stays in the cutter, position the cutter just above the lined cookie sheet. With your finger, gently press the cookie dough to release the cut shape (a).

The dough does not always stay in the cutter, especially as the dough warms to room temperature. If the dough does not stay in the cutter, cut all the shapes, cutting them as close together as possible. After the shapes are cut, use a cookie spatula with a thin blade to transfer the cut shapes to a cookie sheet lined with parchment paper or a silicone mat (b). The cookie dough may stretch or distort if the dough is too warm when cutting. If the dough is well chilled, it is more likely that the dough will stay in the cutter.

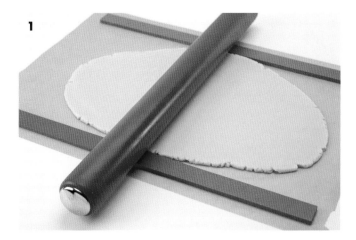

1

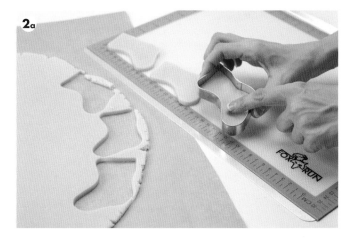

2a

2b

3

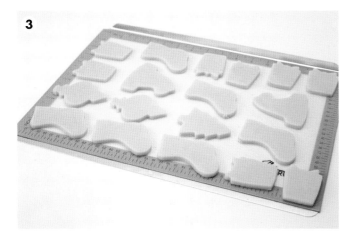

4

3 Place the cookie sheet with the cut shapes in the oven and bake according to the recipe instructions.

4 After the cookies are baked, allow them to cool for 3 to 4 minutes on the cookie sheet. Use a cookie spatula to gently transfer the warm, cut shapes to a cooling rack. Baked cookies will be fragile and soft to touch while they are still hot. Take extra care when moving the baked cookie from the cookie sheet to the cooling rack. Allow the cookies to cool completely before decorating.

Tips for Rolling and Cutting

- Cookie dough may not release easily from cookie cutters with thin or highly detailed shapes. If part of the cookie dough remains in the cutter while part of it releases, dip the cookie cutter in flour before cutting the next cookie. Cutters may be stretched and reshaped slightly if necessary to get the dough to release from a tight area.

- Take the time needed to chill the cookie dough if the recipe calls for chilling. It is frustrating to try and roll soft cookie dough. The dough may be sticky and cutout shapes will be difficult to remove. If the dough is still sticking after chilling, lightly dust flour on the silicone mat, parchment paper, or work surface and on the top of the cookie dough.

- Cookie dough will become overworked if the dough is rolled over and over. The less the dough is rolled, the better. Overworked dough will result in cookies that are very dry and tough, or that have a distorted or shrunken shape. In most cases, I mix the dough and then divide it into two patties. After cutting shapes from the first patty, set the scraps to the side. Roll and cut shapes from the second patty, and again set the scraps to the side. Combine the scraps from both patties and roll. Repeat until no scraps remain. The best shaped cookies will come from the first batches of rolled dough.

- Cut out shapes that are the consistent in size for even baking. Cookies bake best on the center rack of the oven and when one cookie sheet is used. If two cookie sheets are used, space the oven racks evenly and rotate the cookie sheets after 4 to 5 minutes to promote even baking.

- Transfer baked cookies from hot cookie sheets to a cooling rack soon after the cookies are out of the oven to prevent the cookies from browning any further. If the cookies are on a parchment sheet or silicone mat, the sheet or mat can be slid onto the cooling rack. If the cookie sheet is not lined with parchment paper or a silicone baking mat, the baked cookies may stick if left on a hot cookie sheet too long.

ADD A HOLE FOR HANGING

Cut a hole before baking if the cookies will be hung. Cake decorating tip #6 works well for cookies 3" (7.6 cm) and larger. Tip #4 works for cookies smaller than 3" (7.6 cm). It is important to use a cookie recipe that does not rise, or the hole may seal when baked. The cookie recipes included in this book all are ideal for cutting holes. Be careful to avoid underbaking the cookies, or they will not be firm enough to hang.

Inserting Sticks

- Keep in mind the position of the shapes when cutting cookie dough for cookie bouquets. Make sure there is plenty of room for the sticks to protrude from each cut shape. Also consider placement of the sticks. Your oven may not have enough room for sticks placed in every direction.

- If the cookie becomes loose from the stick after baking, add a bit of royal icing or chocolate to the back of the cookie to secure.

ADD A STICK FOR COOKIE BOUQUETS

Create cookie pops or baked cookies on a stick to assemble lovely edible arrangements. When baking cookies on a stick, use a recipe that produces firm cookies to avoid having the cookies break off the stick. To ensure a firm cookie, cool the cookies on a rack so the bottom does not become soft or soggy. Do not underbake the cookies. It is better to have the edges browned slightly than to have a cookie that is underbaked. The cookie recipes included in this book are all ideal for use in bouquets. Use long, paper sticks for the cookies. They may brown slightly. Wrap the sticks with bright ribbons if desired. Plastic sticks may melt in the oven and are not recommended. Wooden sticks may be used but are more difficult to trim to various lengths when arranging a cookie bouquet.

1 Roll the cookie dough using one of the methods on pages 19 or 20. To insert a stick, press the stick into the dough. The end that is inserted into the base of the cookie dough should be resting on the cookie sheet.

2 Hold the other end of the stick between your index finger and thumb. With your dominate hand, begin twisting and pushing the stick up into the cut cookie dough shape. Keep the stick as parallel to the cookie sheet as possible. Use your index finger of your nondominant hand to keep the stick from protruding through the cookie dough. Continue twisting and pushing until the stick is about three-fourths through the cut shape.

Cookie Cutter Shapes

With thousands of cookie cutter shapes available, you can find shapes for nearly all themes and occasions.

If the shape you desire is not available, use these alternatives.

USE YOUR IMAGINATION

Even though a cookie cutter is labeled as a certain shape, it may be used for many other designs. For example, a nutcracker cookie cutter was used for a nutcracker, a robot, and Frankenstein's monster.

Cut the shape and then use additional cutters to remove unwanted cookie dough. For the owl, two common cutters were used: an egg cutter and a round cutter. First the egg shape is cut; then the round cutter is used to remove the top part of the egg, creating a chubby owl.

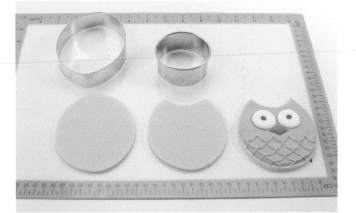

USE A COOKIE CUTTER KIT TO MAKE CUSTOM SHAPES

Keep time-saving, easy-to-use cookie cutter kits on hand for when several shapes need to be cut. If just a few custom shape cookies are needed, make a pattern using cardstock.

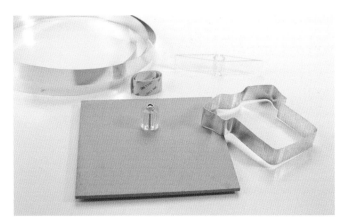

MAKE CARDSTOCK PATTERNS

Use cardstock to make patterns. This works well when only a few cookies need to be cut.

1 Draw or trace the shape desired on a sheet of cardstock. Cut the cardstock. Spray the back side of the cardstock with a grease cooking spray. Place the greased side of the cardstock on the rolled cookie dough.

2 Use a mini–pizza cutter to cut as much as possible, giving the cleanest edge.

3 Use a paring knife to cut any corners.

4 Remove the excess dough. Round any corners by gently pressing on them with your index finger.

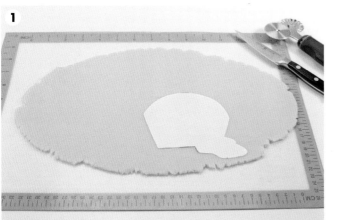

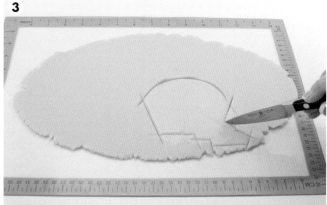

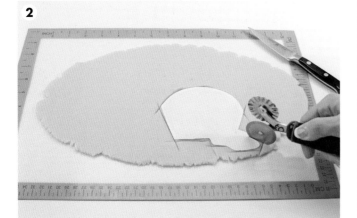

1

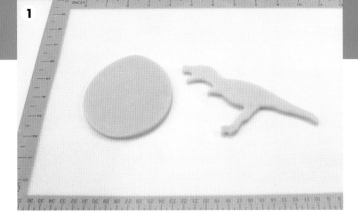

2

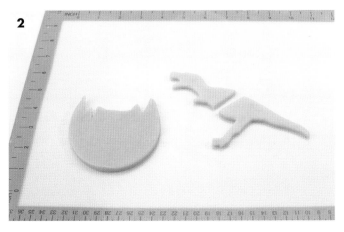

3

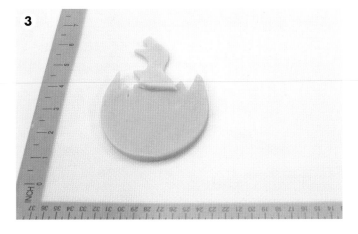

4

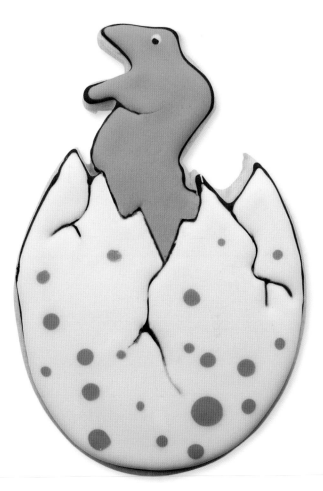

CREATE NEW SHAPES BY COMBINING CUTTERS

You can combine cutter and piece cut shapes together to create a new shape.

1 Cut the two shapes desired.

2 Cut sections of the unbaked shape to accommodate the design. The top one-fourth of the egg was cut and a jagged edge was added. The dinosaur's body was cut.

3 Arrange the two shapes, overlapping the edges.

4 Gently press the cookie dough together to combine the shapes and eliminate the seam.

USE MINI-CUTTERS TO ADD SHAPE

Cut the cookie dough using mini-cutters or aspic cutters to create a design from common shapes. A whimsical cow was created using the body of a gingerbread girl, a circle, and two sizes of teardrop cutters.

REINFORCE THE BACK OF PIECED DOUGH

If the baked cookie has been made using several shapes pieced together, the cookie will be fragile where the shapes adjoin. Once the cookie has cooled, add a little bit of icing on the back to secure the adjoining shapes and prevent the shapes from breaking apart.

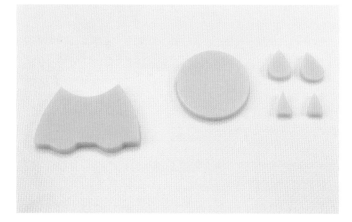

ORGANIZE COOKIE CUTTERS

After collecting dozens of cookie cutters, it can be difficult to find the shape (or even remember what you have). Keep the cutters neatly organized in labeled plastic containers. Keep mini-cutters in a plastic ziplock bag and stored within a plastic container. For even more organization, keep a list of each container's contents. The list should include the cutter design as well as the size. Carry the list whenever shopping for cutters to avoid buying duplicates.

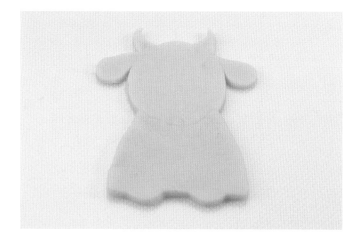

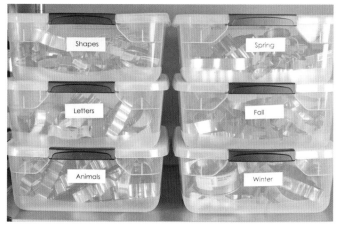

Molding and Stamping Cookie Dough

You can bake a cookie that has dimension and detail by pressing dough. Be sure to use cookie dough that holds its shape when baked when making molded cookies. Traditional molded cookies are made using a Springerle cookie recipe, a classic German cookie recipe. Springerle cookie dough is stamped; then the dough is left to air-dry for several hours. Any of the cookie recipes included in this book will work for molding cookies, though the details will not be as distinct as what can be achieved with the Springerle recipe.

When choosing a mold, look for one that is even in thickness throughout, or the edges may brown before the center is baked. If the mold is highly detailed or too deep, the dough may be difficult to release. Instructions in this chapter are shown using inexpensive hard candy/cookie molds, traditional candy molds, and high-quality, hand-carved wooden mold replicas. Hard candy/cookie molds are great for kids to use, as it is easier to mold than to roll dough. It is also less messy. Simply have kids press in the dough and bake! Hard candy/cookie molds are made of a plastic that withstands heat. Do not confuse these molds with clear candy molds, as these will melt in the oven. Instructions for molding cookies using traditional candy molds are also included, but these molds are a little trickier to use. The candy mold is filled, but the dough is removed before baking. To create a molded cookie using a stamp or hand-carved wooden replica mold, the cookie dough is shaped to fit the stamp, and then the dough is pressed to emboss the design.

The cookie on the left is baked using a Springerle recipe, while the cookie on the right is the buttery sugar cookie recipe.

HARD CANDY/COOKIE MOLDS

1 Lightly spray the cookie mold with a grease cooking spray. Take enough cookie dough to fit into one cavity and roll the dough into a ball. Press the ball into the cavity of the sprayed mold.

2 Press gently to evenly spread the dough.

3 If additional dough is needed, add the dough in the center and press to push the dough to the edges of the mold.

4 Use a paring knife to scrape excess dough from the mold to provide an even surface. Use your index finger to smooth the edges. Continue to step 8 and bake according to directions, or add a stick following steps 5 through 7.

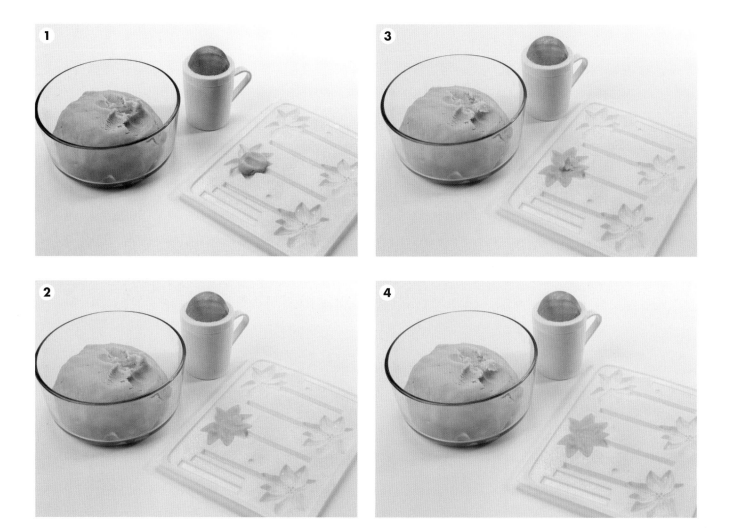

5

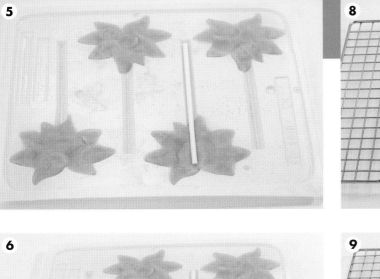

6

7

8

9

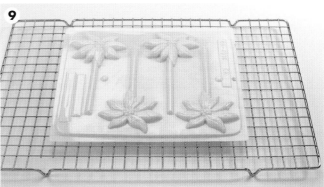

10

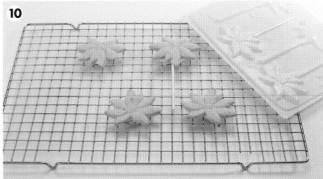

5 The cookies can be baked with or without a sucker stick. If using a sucker stick, place the stick on top of the filled mold, so the stick is extended to nearly the top of the cavity. If desired, cut the mold at the end of each stick cavity to allow longer sticks to extend from the mold.

6 Place a bit of cookie dough on top of the stick.

7 Gently press the dough covering the stick, so it blends in with the dough in the cavity.

8 Place the filled mold on a cookie sheet. Bake in a 325°F (160°C) oven (this may be lower than the recipe temperature). Bake for 10 to 12 minutes or until the edges begin to turn golden. Remove the cookie sheet from the oven and allow to cool for a few minutes. Place a cooling rack upside down on top of the mold. Although the type of plastic in the mold will not melt when heated at temperatures 325°F (160°C) and below, the plastic will warp if handled while the mold is still warm. Allow the mold to cool on the cookie sheet for a few minutes before placing the cooling rack on top.

9 Using both hands, grip the cooling rack and the hard candy mold. Flip over the cooling rack and the mold at the same time. Lift the mold. If the cookies do not release when the mold is lifted, gently flex the mold.

10 Allow the cookies to cool completely before decorating.

CLEAR CANDY MOLDS

1 Lightly spray the candy mold with a grease cooking spray. Dust the candy mold with flour. Take enough cookie dough to fit into one cavity and roll the dough into a ball. Press the ball into the cavity of the sprayed mold. Press gently to evenly spread the dough.

2 Use a paring knife to scrape excess dough from the mold to provide an even surface. Use your index finger to smooth along the edges. Continue to directions in step 6, or add a stick following directions 3 to 5.

3 The cookies can be baked with or without a sucker stick. If using a sucker stick, place the sucker stick on top of the filled mold, making sure that the stick is extended to nearly the top of the cavity. If desired, cut the mold at the end of each stick cavity to allow longer sticks to extend from the mold.

4 Place a bit of cookie dough on top of the stick.

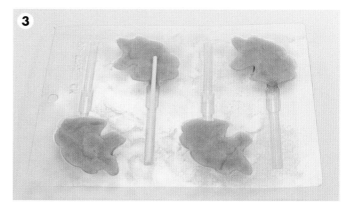

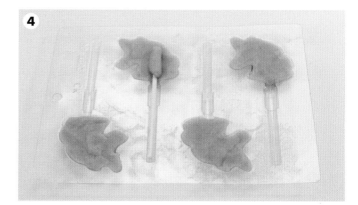

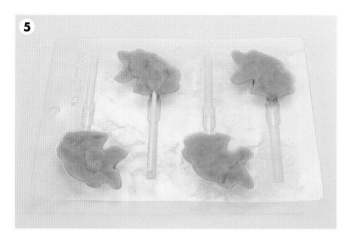

5 Gently press the dough covering the stick, so it blends with the new dough in the cavity.

6 Place the filled mold in the freezer for about 15 minutes. When the dough is chilled, gently press on the cavity to release the frozen cookie dough. Place the frozen dough on a cookie sheet lined with parchment paper or a silicone baking mat. Wait a few minutes to allow the cookies to return to room temperature.

If the dough does not release from the mold, return the filled mold to the freezer for a few more minutes. If the dough still does not release, the mold may not have been dusted with enough flour. Allow the mold to warm to room temperature and remove the dough. Generously spray again with a cooking spray and thoroughly dust with flour. If the dough still does not release, the mold may be too detailed or deep for the dough.

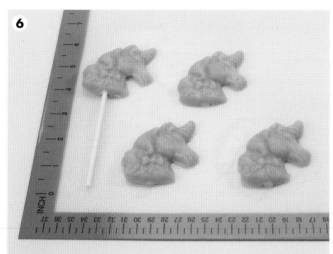

7 Bake according to recipe instructions or until the edges begin to turn golden. Use a cookie spatula to gently transfer the warm, molded shapes to a cooling rack. Baked cookies will be fragile and soft to touch while they are still hot. Take extra care when moving the baked cookie from the cookie sheet to the cooling rack. Allow the cookies to cool completely before decorating.

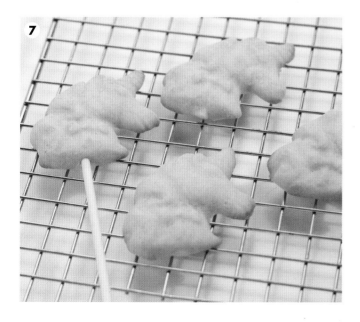

WOODEN COOKIE MOLDS

1 Mix cookie dough and chill if required by the recipe. Allow the chilled dough to return to room temperature. Generously brush the wooden replica mold with powdered sugar or flour. Take a small amount of cookie dough and flatten to the size of the mold. In most cases, the flattened shape should be about the thickness of the wooden mold, or approximately ½" (1.3 cm) thick. Place the flattened dough on a cookie sheet lined with parchment paper or a silicone baking mat.

2 Firmly and evenly press the shape with the cookie mold to emboss the design.

3 Use a mini–pizza cutter to trim around the mold. Some of the molds may have a hanger for decorative purposes. Do not trim the side of the mold with the hanger.

4 Lift the mold.

5 Trim the side of the dough where the hanger was. If using a Springerle recipe, allow the dough to dry and bake according to the recipe directions. Otherwise, bake according to recipe instructions or until the edges begin to turn golden. Use a cookie spatula to gently transfer the warm, molded shapes to a cooling rack. Baked cookies will be fragile and soft to touch while they are still hot. Take extra care when removing the baked cookie from the cookie sheet to the cooling rack. Allow the cookies to cool completely before decorating.

Cookie cutters may be used in place of a mini–pizza cutter. Stamp the shape, lift the mold, and cut using the cookie cutter.

COOKIE STAMPS

1 Mix cookie dough and chill if required by the recipe. Allow the chilled dough to return to room temperature. Lightly spray the stamp with a grease cooking spray. Take a small amount of cookie dough and roll the dough into a ball. The ball should be about half the size of the stamp's design. Place the rolled cookie dough ball on a cookie sheet lined with parchment paper or a silicone baking mat. Place additional rolled balls on the baking mat, allowing room for the dough to extend when stamped.

2 Firmly and evenly press the ball with the cookie stamp to emboss the design. Lift the stamp.

Dough Sticking

If the dough sticks to the mold or stamp when lifting, gently nudge your fingers all along the edges to release the dough. If the dough is still sticking, knead a bit more flour into the cookie dough.

3 Leaving the edge as is after stamping gives the cookie a rustic finish. If cleaner edges are desired, cut the stamped dough with a round cookie cutter.

4 Transfer the silicone baking mat or parchment paper to a cookie sheet. Bake the cookies according to the recipe directions.

5 Use a cookie spatula to gently transfer the warm, molded shapes to a cooling rack. Baked cookies will be fragile and soft to touch while they are still hot. Take extra care when moving the baked cookie from the cookie sheet to the cooling rack. Allow the cookies to cool completely before decorating.

COOKIE ICINGS

The following section covers several types of icings and the tools needed to decorate cookies. Icing recipes and instructions in this section include royal icing, run sugar, buttercream, rolled fondant, egg wash, and candy coating. Each chapter covers recipes, icing application, and storage. Some of the icing techniques can be combined. For instance, rolled fondant–covered cookies are often enhanced with royal icing-piped designs. Also included in this section is a chart for time management. A decorating chart helps you choose the icing best suited for your needs, whether you are looking for a cookie with the best taste, one for decorating with kids, or cookies that ship well.

Decorating Tools and Edible Decorations

The tools you'll need for cookie decorating vary depending on the icing. Pastry bags and tips are used for run sugar and buttercream or any icing that requires piping. Rolling pins, gum paste cutters, and extruders are used for rolled fondant–covered cookies. There are lots of edible decorations that give quick color and dimension to the cookie.

STAND MIXER

A stand mixer is helpful when mixing icings. Mixing royal icing to the proper consistency requires blending the ingredients on medium to high for several minutes. This can be exhausting if using a hand mixer. Buttercream, on the other hand, is mixed on low for only a few minutes, so a hand mixer is more appropriate for this icing.

PASTRY BAGS AND PARCHMENT CONES

Several sizes and materials are available. Choose a reusable bag that is thin, lightweight, and conforms to your hand when squeezed. Disposable bags are convenient for cleanup. A 12" (30.5 cm) disposable or reusable bag is a standard size for decorating. Smaller bags are easier to control but need to be refilled more often. Larger bags are more difficult to control but hold more icing. Use pastry bag ties or twisties to keep icing from spilling out of the bag. Bag ties and twisties are especially helpful when decorating cookies with kids. You can also create a homemade disposable bag from a triangle of parchment. Parchment cones are ideal for quick cleanup. Simply remove the tip and toss the bag when finished decorating. Stands to hold filled pastry bags are available at cake and candy supply stores. These stands are also handy for filling pastry bags with icing, allowing both hands to be free to fill the bag. Tall drinking glasses can be used as well. Some pastry stands include a sponge on which the pastry tip rests, which keeps the icing in the tip from hardening.

PASTRY TIPS AND COUPLERS

A variety of pastry tips are used for piping. Run sugar icing requires small, round-opening tips. It is handy to have several small round-opening tips so you won't need to wash the tip when switching piping colors. PME Supatubes are superior to standard metal tips. They are stainless steel, seamless, and have precise openings. The PME numbers vary slightly from standard tip numbers. Choose PME Supatubes #0, #1, #1.5, #2, #2.5, #3, and #4. Buttercream icing will hold its shape when piped and there are several tips to create fun piped designs. Larger round openings, such as tip #6, #8 or #10, are used to pipe figures on the cookie. Leaf tips #350 and #352 make nice leaves for Christmas trees and wreaths. Multiple small round opening tip #233 is ideal to create fur or grass. Tip #46 is used to make bows and stripes. A coupler is a two-part tool that allows you to change the tip and use the same pastry bag. A tip cleaning brush is an invaluable tool for cleaning up. The small cylinder shape is designed to reach the hard-to-clean points of tips.

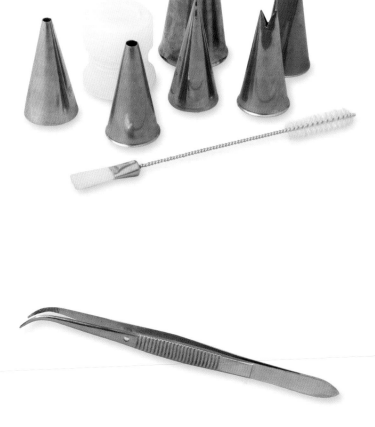

TWEEZERS

Tweezers are essential when attaching small edible decorations, eliminating possible finger marks.

BRUSHES

An assortment of round and flat brushes are useful for nearly all the icings used in this book. Reserve a set of brushes to use exclusively with food. Brushes with round bristles that come to a fine taper are ideal for painting details on run sugar, rolled fondant, candy coating, and egg wash glaze. A flat brush is used for brush embroidery. Flat brushes are also used to remove excess sugars or particles when flocking on cookies. Round brushes with large, soft bristles are used to apply dusting powders. Pastry brushes are used to apply piping gel onto cookies to attach rolled fondant.

FOOD COLOR

Gel, liquid, and powder are the most common forms of food color. Information about each of the types and how to use them can be found on page 51.

FOOD COLOR MARKERS

Markers filled with food color are used to color details on any icing that forms a firm crust such as rolled fondant or run sugar. Several companies manufacture markers with a wide spectrum of colors and tip sizes. Keep a set of fine-tip markers on hand as well as markers that have a broad tip.

DUSTING POWDERS

There are a few types of dusting powders. The powders can be brushed on cookies in powder form for an all-over application. Mix with grain alcohol to create a paint. Luster dusts, platinum dusts, and pearl dusts have a shimmer and are available in many metallic colors including gold, silver, copper, and pearl. Super pearl is one of the most useful powders, as it can be brushed on any color to create a white-metallic sheen. It looks best when brushed on cookies with white or pastel icings. Petal dusts have a matte finish and work well to shade accent pieces such as flowers, for a realistic-looking accent. Some dusts are not yet FDA approved and should be used for decoration only.

SUGARS

Sugars add a sparkle when applied to cookie icings. Sanding sugar is more coarse than granulated sugar and provides more sparkle. Coarse sugar is more coarse than sanding sugar and may look heavy on small cookies. White coarse or sanding sugar can be colored to create custom shades to match cookies. Follow directions on page 133 to color sugar.

SPRINKLES

Add a touch of color and create a theme using the wide variety of edible sprinkles and confetti available. For example, edible confetti in the shape of snowflakes, gingerbread boys, or candy canes can add instant decorations to simple iced cookies.

EDIBLE GLITTER AND EDIBLE GLITTER DUST

Edible glitter is small edible flakes that offer a subtle sparkle under light. Edible glitter is available in flakes or in an extra-fine powder, called edible glitter dust. Edible glitter and edible glitter dust do not add flavor or texture.

DISCO DUST

Disco dust, sometimes called fairy dust, creates the most sparkly effect; it is non-toxic but not yet FDA approved for consumption. Disco dust is recommended to use on cookies that will be used only as decoration and not for consumption.

EDIBLE ROUND CANDIES

Round balls of sugar, available in a variety of colors and sizes, provide instant dimension and color. Nonpareils are tiny balls used as an all-over application on a cookie. Sugar pearls or candy beads range in size from 2 mm to 7 mm. Sixlets are larger, approximately 10 mm. Nonpareils, sugar pearls, and candy beads are all sugar-sweetened balls with a hard shell. Sixlets have chocolate inside with a candy shell. Some of the round candies are available with a pearl finish, giving a subtle sheen.

METALLIC DRAGÉES

Spheres, diamonds, ovals, and other shapes of sugar-coated candies with a metallic finish are striking on cookies. However, the United States Food and Drug Administration (FDA) classifies silver or gold dragées as nonedible products that are sold for decorative purposes only. In other countries, including the United Kingdom, they are classed as food items. An FDA-approved alternative to dragées are balls in gold, silver, white, and other colors with a pearl sheen. The pearl finish is not as spectacular as the metallic, but it is a nice substitute.

METALLIC EDIBLE SPRAYS

Sprays in an aerosol provide instant metallic colors to iced cookies. These edible sprays are available in popular sheens like pearl, gold, and silver.

LARGE SUGAR OR ROYAL ICING EDIBLE DECORATIONS

Icing decorations are made by piping royal icing onto parchment paper to create designs. Royal icing shapes can be handmade or purchased. Royal icing edible eyes, in several sizes, are available premade to quickly add eyes to cookies. Molded sugar pieces are also available in a variety of designs.

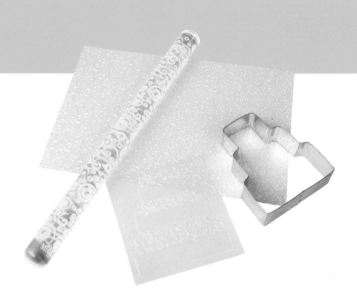

PIPING GEL

Piping gel is a clear, flavorless gel used to attach edible decorations to cookies. Decorations can be placed on the cookie while the icing is wet, or piping gel may be used as a glue to attach the decorations. Piping gel may be brushed on baked cookies to attach rolled fondant. It is also used when flocking cookies as well. Piping gel comes in a tub or a squeeze tube.

TEXTURE MATS AND TEXTURE ROLLING PINS

Texture mats and texture rolling pins add an instant all-over pattern to rolled fondant. Cookie cutters with coordinating texture mats are available for quick decorating.

GUM PASTE AND ROLLED FONDANT CUTTERS

Add cut decorations using gum paste and rolled fondant cutters. These cutters are typically smaller than cookie cutters so they are excellent to use for small accents on iced cookies. Many of the cutters, such as patchwork cutters, have details embossed for simple decorating.

SPATULAS

Cake decorating spatulas, which have a long, thin metal blade, are used to mix and color icing. When spreading icing onto a cookie, use a small, straight spatula. Icing easily glides across the cookie's surface. Using the side of the spatula along the side of a cookie cleans up the cookie's edge. Spatulas or palette knives with a thin, tapered blade are used for lifting rolled fondant accents and placing them on the cookie.

SQUEEZE BOTTLE

Lightweight squeeze bottles are used for piping with chocolate or candy coating. Squeeze bottles can also be used with run sugar, but the run sugar must be thin or it is difficult to squeeze the icing from the bottle. If the icing is too thin, it will drip off the sides of the cookie. Fill a squeeze bottle with sanding sugar to easily control the flow when applying sugar to icing for flocking, page 138.

TOOTHPICKS

Toothpicks are used to remove food color from jars. Always start with a clean toothpick when dipping into the jar; reusing the toothpick may contaminate the food color in the jar. Toothpicks are also handy to coax run sugar icing into small areas or corners.

SCISSORS

Sharp kitchen scissors are useful for trimming off the point in parchment bags and creating tiny openings. Scissors are also used to trim the edges of cookies dipped in candy coating.

CLAY GUN/EXTRUDER

These extruders are used to make even gum paste or rolled fondant lines and ropes with consistent thickness. The extruder kits include a variety of interchangeable disks.

CUTTING TOOLS

A CelBoard is a perfectly smooth and flat surface on which you can place small pieces of rolled fondant or gum paste for cutting. A CelFlap is a clear sheet that is placed on top of rolled gum paste or fondant to keep pieces from drying.

The mini–pizza cutter is a handy tool for trimming cookie dough. This tool is also invaluable when cutting strips and pieces of fondant or gum paste. Use a stainless steel ruler to ensure cut strips are straight. The PolyBlade is a thin, flexible blade made of stainless steel. Because it is so thin, it will make micro-thin cuts without crushing the rolled fondant or gum paste. A pair of small scissors is used for snipping small, precise cuts in gum paste and fondant. A paring knife is used in many ways for decorating. A bench scraper is a tool with a large, flat blade and a handle. Use this tool for cutting through large chunks of fondant and gum paste. The bench scraper is also handy for cleanup. Hold the blade at a 45° angle and scrape the work surface to remove crusted pieces of gum paste or fondant.

MODELING TOOLS

A set of modeling tools is essential for embossing cookies and is helpful for other projects. A basic starter kit should include ball tools in a variety of sizes, a tool with a cone at the end, a veining tool, and a dog bone tool. Other practical tools include a quilting wheel, shell tool, and scribing needle. CelSticks are a handy modeling tool used for many applications. These sticks have a rounded end and a tapered, pointed end. CelSticks are the best tools to use for frilling and adding ruffles. Toothpicks are much more difficult to control.

FOAM

Foam sheets and pads are used for cupping flowers. Many double-sided foam pads are used with nonstick rolling pins to manipulate rolled fondant shapes. One side of the foam is soft, while the other side is firm. Use the soft side for frilling (page 168). The firm side may be used for rolling and cutting. Some foam pads have holes for drying and shaping flowers.

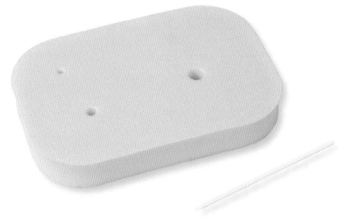

MOLDS

Molds are an efficient way to decorate. Silicone molds are flexible, highly detailed, and allow rolled fondant and gum paste to be easily released from the molds. Elegant lace and strands of beads can be made from silicone molds. Inexpensive candy molds can be used and almost any theme may be found. Other molds can be found in craft stores; be sure to check that any mold you use is food grade.

PASTA MACHINE

A pasta machine can be a costly investment, but it is well worth the price for cookie decorating alone. Freestanding machines that crank the fondant are available, or attachments exist for mixers such as a KitchenAid. Generally, flowers and accents on cookies should be rolled very thin, such as setting #5 on a KitchenAid pasta attachment. An alternative to a pasta machine is a set of perfection strips. Roll gum paste or fondant between the two perfection strips of the same thickness. The gum paste is rolled with an even thickness, not getting any thinner than the strips. Although these strips will not produce rolled fondant or gum paste as thin as a pasta machine does, they can be used with projects that do not require a thin sheet of gum paste.

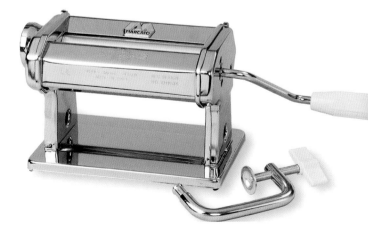

Decorating Chart

The icings in the book each have different working characteristics, distinctive flavors, and unique appearances. The decorating chart may help determine which icing is best suited for your particular needs and desires. The icings each have an entire chapter devoted to working with the icing as well as additional information. The chart contains general guidelines and estimates using the icings that are detailed in the subsequent chapters. Much of it is subjective. The pictures of the duck cookies represents how the finished cookies will look.

Run Sugar, page 64

Painted Run Sugar, page 78

Buttercream Icing, page 82

Rolled Fondant, page 100

Chocolate Coated, page 114

Egg Wash Glaze, page 120

COOKIE STAR RATING

	GOOD FOR DECORATING WITH KIDS	FLAVOR	SHIPPING	HOLDS UP IN HEAT	FREEZING
Buttercream	✪✪✪✪✪	✪✪✪✪✪	✪	✪	✪✪
Chocolate	✪✪✪	✪✪✪✪✪	✪	✪	✪✪✪✪
Run Sugar	✪✪	✪✪✪	✪✪✪✪✪	✪✪✪✪	✪
Painted Run Sugar	✪✪✪✪✪	✪✪✪	✪✪✪✪✪	✪✪✪	✪
Egg Wash Glaze	✪✪✪✪✪	✪✪	✪✪✪✪✪	✪✪✪	✪
Rolled Fondant	✪✪✪	✪✪✪✪	✪✪✪	✪✪✪✪	✪✪

FLAVOR

Of course flavor is completely subjective. I have based the star rating on my personal favorite as well as a poll I've taken of those who have eaten many of my creations.

Run sugar is made by thinning royal icing with water. It provides subtle sweetness with a bit of crunch. The flavor can be enhanced with extracts.

My favorite icing may vary from day to day, but I typically love cookies iced with buttercream. The very sweet icing is creamy, delicious, and soft when bitten.

Some people are hesitant to try rolled fondant on a cookie. While I personally do not love the flavor and texture of rolled fondant on a cake, I do enjoy the chewy sweetness on the cookie recipes in this book.

Using chocolate or candy coatings is a delicious way to ice cookies. Oil-based flavors or concentrated flavors can be added for even more options.

Cookies glazed with egg wash provide minimal sweetness.

DECORATING WITH KIDS

The star rating in this category is based on my experience. I have four kids; each has decorated dozens of cookies using all the icings in the book. Most older children, those age twelve and up, can decorate cookies using any of the icings. Younger children may have a tougher time controlling pastry bags. Be sure to secure all pastry bags with twist ties, rubber bands, or icing bag ties to keep icing from spilling out of the bag.

Kids can use run sugar icing, but it tends to be a bit messy. Using squeeze bottles will eliminate some of the mess, though it may be difficult for children to squeeze. Water may be added to the run sugar before filling the squeeze bottles to make the squeezing a little easier, but the icing may drip off the cookie. Painted run sugar is a good choice when decorating with kids. Have the cookies iced and completely set with white run sugar before bringing the kids in. Then let them color on the details with food color markers.

Buttercream is a fun icing for kids because you can achieve numerous textures with it. The icing is not as thin as run sugar or chocolate, making it easier for kids to handle the bags. Watch kids carefully, they love to squeeze the icing right into their mouths!

Rolled fondant is another great medium for children to use. This edible playdough can be molded, cut, or hand shaped. Remind the kids to keep the rolled fondant covered when it is not being used, or it will become dry and crumbly.

Kids also love working with chocolate or candy coating. Simply pour melted candy coating into a squeeze bottle, or let the kids decorate the cookies with candy writers. Chocolate transfer sheets are available in many fun prints. Children can't wait for the chocolate to set so they can peel back the chocolate transfer sheet and see the awesome printed design on their cookies. The disadvantage of chocolate is the mess. Chocolate flows easily from the squeeze bottle, so it can drip all over if care is not taken. Cover the work surface with parchment paper to keep cleanup minimal.

Molded cookies that are glazed with egg wash can be another exciting, edible project for kids. Even very young children can help with the baking and decorating process. They can press the cookie dough into the molds, bake the dough, glaze the baked and cooled cookies, and then color in the details with food markers. The glaze requires time to dry before the details can be colored.

SHIPPING

Run sugar is the best icing to use if the cookies will be shipped. They hold up well in warmer and colder temperatures. The cookies dry with a hard finish, which makes them suitable for stacking.

Buttercream icing forms a crust on the outside but is soft on the inside, which makes these cookies difficult to ship. Decorations may become smashed. Buttercream is a shortening-based icing that will melt in warmer temperatures.

Cookies that are covered with rolled fondant ship nicely if the rolled fondant covering is flat without dimension. It is important to allow the rolled fondant to form a firm coating overnight before packaging. Dainty flowers or other three-dimensional accents made of rolled fondant are delicate, so cookies with such decorations are likely to arrive with broken pieces. If the only dimension on the cookie is a textured piece of rolled fondant, the cookie should be okay to ship.

Chocolate- or candy-coated cookies ship fine if the weather is not too warm. The coating dries completely, making them ideal for stacking. Treat the chocolate- or candy-coated cookie as you would a candy bar that melts in warm temperatures. Keep in mind, the inside of shipping carriers reaches much hotter temperatures than the temperature outdoors.

Egg wash glaze dries completely, so these cookies ship well.

FREEZING

Humidity is the main deterrent when freezing cookies. Moisture may cause colors in buttercream icing and run sugar to bleed or develop tiny moisture spots. Rolled fondant–covered cookies may also spot with the presence of moisture. Chocolate- or candy-coated cookies freeze beautifully if the cookies are properly packaged; if not, they will become tacky to touch.

Baked cookies that are not decorated freeze beautifully. Allow the frozen cookies to come to room temperature before decorating. If baked cookies or decorated cookies must be frozen ahead of time, be sure to follow the following freezer packaging instructions. Place cookies in a container. If the cookies will not lose detail when stacked, they can be stacked with sheets of parchment between each layer. Wrap the container with two layers of plastic wrap; then wrap the container with foil. Place the container in the freezer. When the wrapped box is removed from the freezer, allow the cookies to warm to room temperature before unwrapping the plastic wrap and foil.

Cookie Decorating Design and Planning

Often the theme and colors of a party or event determine the decorating. If you're preparing cookies for a party, coordinate the decorations to match the party tableware and decorations. If the cookies are a stand-alone treat, the Internet is a valuable source for color combinations, cookie designs, and ideas. For inspiration, type the theme in your computer's web browser and add the word "clipart." A plethora of possibilities await you!

DESIGNING THE COOKIE

Before piping icing onto the cookie, plan the inside design. Place the cookie cutter on a sheet of paper, and outline it with a pencil. Then draw the design inside the outline. For additional visualization, color the drawing. Coloring may seem like unnecessary extra work, but it provides a helpful visual of all the colors that will be used. There have been many times that I have discarded colored icing, only to find out I needed the color later! When I don't have time to color my design with colored pencils, I still make a list of the colors needed for each cookie.

The Internet can also help when planning the inside design of your shape. For example, when decorating an outline of a dog sitting, you may have trouble visualizing where the legs extend. Simply type in "sitting dog clipart" in your browser; and view the resulting images for ideas.

TIME MANAGEMENT

With all methods of cookie decorating, it is most efficient to decorate in an assembly line. Decorate the same detail on each of the cookies before moving to the next detail. This will not only make the decorating process faster, it allows time for the first detail to dry or crust before adding the adjoining detail. When planning the baking and decorating process, be sure to allow enough time for the dough to chill, baked cookies to cool, and decorated cookies to dry. This means that, while possible, baking and decorating is not just a one-day process. The icing drying time will vary depending on the type of icing used. For example, chocolate-coated cookies can be baked, coated in chocolate, and packaged within one day, whereas run sugar cookies can be baked and iced in one day but should not be packaged until the next.

Coloring and Flavoring Icings

Food color is available in many forms to brighten and color icings. Colors are available in jars, squeeze bottles, or tubes. Gel, paste, powder, and liquid are the most common forms of food color. Gel and paste colors are the most popular. They are water based and highly concentrated. Concentrated colors are the best to use as they will give the most vibrant color without affecting the consistency of the icing.

Powdered food colors are also highly concentrated. It is best to dissolve the powdered granules before mixing the color into the icing, or dark speckles may appear. Dissolve the powdered granules in a small amount of water before mixing the color with royal icing. For buttercream and rolled fondant, blend a small amount of vegetable shortening with the powdered color. Liquid color can be found at the grocery stores. Liquid color is best suited for pastel colors as dark colors are difficult to obtain. Too much liquid color may affect the consistency of the icing. Oil-based colors are used in coloring chocolates and coatings. Liquid, gel, and paste colors are water-based and may cause the chocolate or candy coating to seize or become too firm.

It is not necessary to have every color available. A cabinet full of icing colors can be overwhelming, messy, and take up a lot of space. Red, yellow, and blue are the only colors you really need to mix all other colors. However, it is inconvenient and sometimes difficult to create the colors you want. Keeping a jar of each of the primary colors (red, blue, and yellow), secondary colors (purple, green, and orange), pink, black, and brown will provide a nice assortment for nearly every color palette.

Every brand of food color varies. For example, some reds appear orange, while others look dark pink. AmeriColor food colors provide wonderful, vibrant color and come in bottles that are easy to squeeze. If only a small amount of color is needed, use a toothpick to remove the color from the container, as the color in the squeeze bottles tends to release in large bursts. Here are the AmeriColor colors that I keep on hand: super red, orange, yellow, leaf green, sky blue, violet, black, chocolate brown, deep pink, white, and ivory. I also love the bright, vibrant colors of the electric color line from this company (electric pink, electric yellow, etc). The brightest icings are made using the electric colors. Nearly all the cookies decorated in this book use these eleven basic colors or the electric colors.

Deep shades such as red, black, purple, and royal blue darken as they set. If possible, mix a lighter shade of these colors the night before you decorate and then just add more color if needed. Darker colors also may make the icing bitter as well as leave a tinge of coloring on the cookie eater's mouth. When you want a black or brown color, try adding cocoa powder to the icing to obtain a deep shade with a pleasant taste before adding black or brown food color.

Keep decorated cookies covered after decorating, or the colors may fade. Natural sunlight and fluorescent lights are the harshest on colored icings, but common household lighting may also cause colors to fade.

THE COLOR WHEEL

The color wheel is a useful tool when coloring icing. It can help you when creating custom colors—if a shade is not quite right, use the wheel to help determine what color to add. Understanding the color wheel will also help in deciding which colors complement each other when choosing colors for the cookies.

Primary Colors

Red, yellow, and blue are the primary colors. These are the colors that cannot be made by combining other colors. All other colors are derived from these three colors.

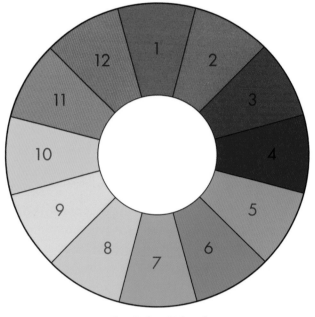

The Color Wheel

Secondary Colors

Orange, green, and purple are the secondary colors. They are achieved by mixing two primary colors together. For example, red (1) and yellow (9) make orange (11).

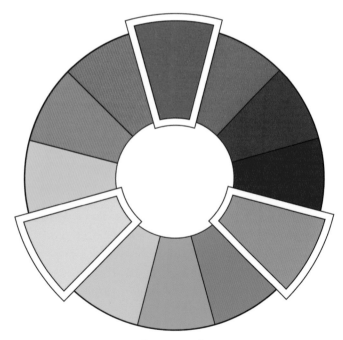

Primary Colors

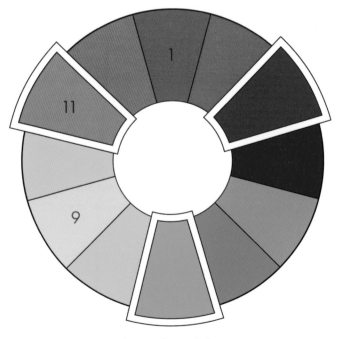

Secondary Colors

Opposites on the Color Wheel

Opposite colors are across from one another on the color wheel. Opposite colors create the maximum contrast and are complementary. The opposite color of any primary color is made by combining the other two primary colors. The result is the primary's complementary, or opposite color. Opposites are very helpful when mixing exact shades. For example, if brown icing looks "too green," add a bit of the opposite color, which would be red.

Analogous Colors

Analogous colors are next to each other on the color wheel. These colors are in harmony with one another.

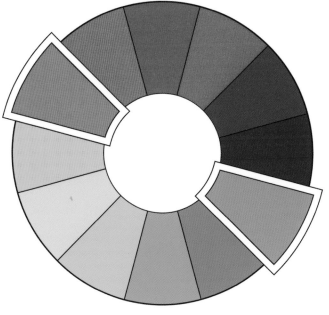

Opposites

Tertiary Colors

Tertiary colors are subtle color combinations created by mixing the primary and secondary adjacent color on the color wheel. For example, you would get a teal (6) by mixing blue (5) and green (7).

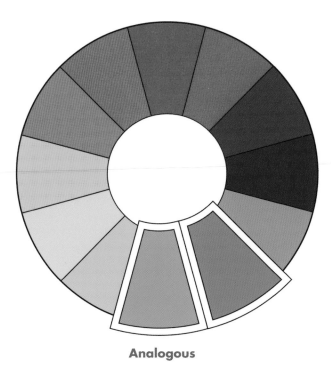

Analogous

Noncolors

Black and white are not considered true colors on the color wheel. Black can be made by mixing red, yellow, and blue food colors. However, mixing black is difficult and requires a large amount of food color, so it is best to purchase black food color.

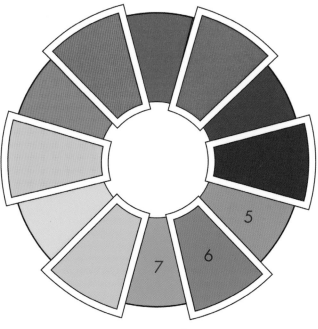

Tertiary Colors

COLORING ICING

1 Before mixing color, ensure that all icing ingredients are thoroughly combined.

2 Add a small amount of food color to the icing. Use a toothpick for color in jars; if the color is in tubes, squeeze the color into the icing.

3 Blend until all color is thoroughly combined and no streaks of color are visible. If the color is too dark, add white icing. If the color is too light, add a little more color.

Coloring Icing

- Color a little more icing than you think you'll need. It is difficult to duplicate the exact shade if you run out.

- To avoid getting the icing too dark, begin by coloring a small amount of icing and then add it to rest of the icing. This will also make blending the icing easier with fewer streaks.

- When creating a custom color, experiment with a small amount of icing and food color before coloring the full amount needed for the project. This will help you avoid ending up with an undesirable color and wasting ingredients.

1

2

3

FLAVORING ICINGS

Change or enhance the flavor of your icing with one of dozens of flavorings and extracts that are available. Extracts are most commonly used in icing recipes, but emulsions or concentrated flavors and oils may be substituted. Concentrated flavors and oils are about three times stronger than extracts, so add approximately one-third the flavoring called for in the recipe. Some flavors may affect the color of the icing. Choose clear flavors when available. If purchasing commercially made icings, simply add the flavor to taste. If mixing the recipe from scratch, replace any flavoring in the recipe with the flavor desired. Start with a small amount and add to taste.

Flavor Caution

Flavoring or ingredients containing acid, such as lemon juice, may alter the color.

Using Pastry Bags, Parchment Cones, and Squeeze Bottles

A pastry bag, parchment cone, or squeeze bottle holds the icing. A pastry bag or parchment cone will conform to your hand, making it easy to control the flow of icing for piped designs. A parchment bag is made by shaping a parchment triangle into a cone. Tips may be dropped into the parchment bags or pastry bags without a coupler, or a coupler may be used to change tips without filling a new bag. Cleanup is easier using a parchment cone or disposable pastry bag. Simply snip off the end of the bag, remove the tip, and dispose of the bag. The only cleaning required is the tip. A squeeze bottle is a great tool for children or for coating a cookie with candy coating. A squeeze bottle can also be used with run sugar, however, it is difficult to squeeze if the run sugar is too thick. If the run sugar icing is too thin, it will be easier to squeeze but will likely drip down the side of the cookie. A pastry bag or parchment cone is required for buttercream and stiff royal icing, as these icings are too stiff for a squeeze bottle.

FILLING A SQUEEZE BOTTLE

Mix icing or melt candy coating in a bowl with a spout or a squared edge. Pour the icing or candy coating into the squeeze bottle. Screw on the cap. Cut the tip of the cap if the opening is too small.

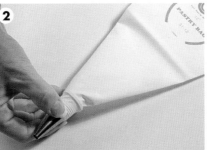

FITTING A BAG WITH A COUPLER

1 Cut the reusable pastry bag or disposable pastry bag so that one or two threads are showing on the coupler base when the coupler base is dropped into the bag. Pull the coupler tightly to secure.

2 Place a tip on the coupler base.

3 Twist the coupler screw top to tighten the tip in place.

USING A BAG
WITHOUT A COUPLER

A tip can be dropped into a bag without a coupler. Cut the bag so that the bottom third of the tip protrudes from the pastry bag.

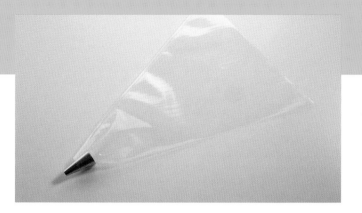

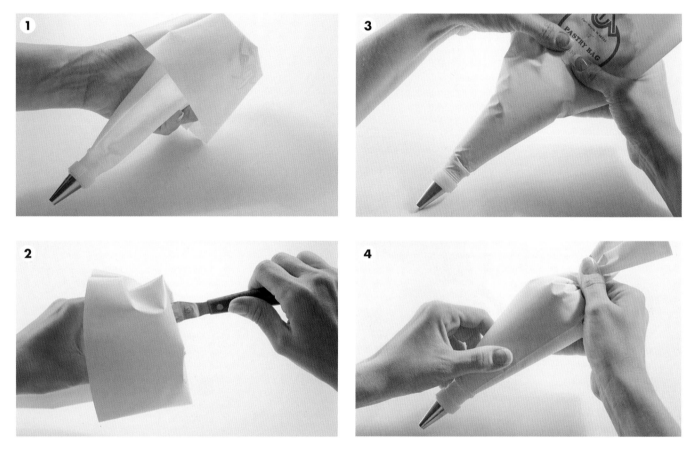

FILLING REUSABLE AND
DISPOSABLE PASTRY BAGS

1 Drop the tip into the pastry bag and tug on the end to secure. The bag may also be fitted with a coupler following the instructions on page 55. Fold the pastry bag over your hands to form a cuff. The cuff fold should be 2" to 3" (5.1 to 7.6 cm). For ease in filling, the bag can be placed in a tall drinking glass or a pastry bag holder with the cuff folded over.

2 Scoop icing into the bag until it reaches the top of the cuff. Fill the bag about half full with icing. The fuller the bag, the more difficult the bag is to control.

3 Unfold the cuff. Squeeze the bag between your thumb and fingers and push the icing toward the bottom of the bag.

4 Twist the bag where the icing begins. If desired, secure with a rubber band, twist tie, or icing bag tie to ensure that the icing doesn't burst from the top of the bag.

Air Bubbles

Each time pastry bags are refilled, there is a buildup of air. Before beginning to pipe again, squeeze the pastry bag to release the trapped air; otherwise a large air bubble will interrupt the piping.

MAKING A PARCHMENT CONE

Parchment paper is available in precut triangles. Use these triangles to create pastry bags that are lightweight, inexpensive, and disposable. If a parchment cone is well made, a tip may not be needed when a round opening is desired. Simply cut the tapered end of the parchment cone to the size needed.

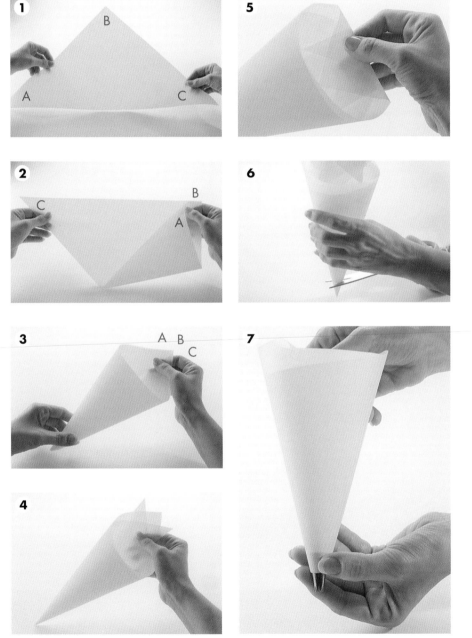

1 The triangle is labeled A, B, and C.

2 Fold corner A to meet corner B, twisting to form a cone.

3 Fold corner C to meet corner B, keeping the cone shape with a tight point. Align all three points.

4 Cross over corners A and C, making a "W" to ensure the seams of the cone overlap. Always keep the bottom point tight. Shift A and C up and down to further ensure a tight point.

5 Fold in the corners to secure the bag, or secure the seam with tape.

6 Cut the parchment bag at the point, large enough so one-third of a tip will protrude from the bag.

7 Drop the tip, narrow end first into the bag. If more than one-third of the tip is showing, the tip may pop out of the bag during piping.

FILLING PARCHMENT CONES

1 Hold the parchment bag and fill halfway with icing.

2 Squeeze the bag between your thumb and fingers to fill the bottom of the bag.

3 Fold in the left side, then the right side. Fold down the middle, and continue to fold until you reach the top of the icing.

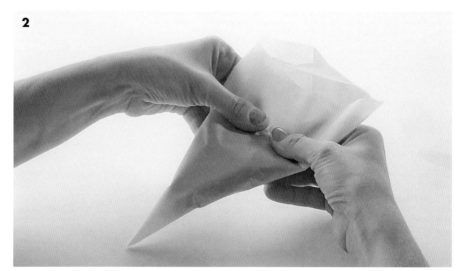

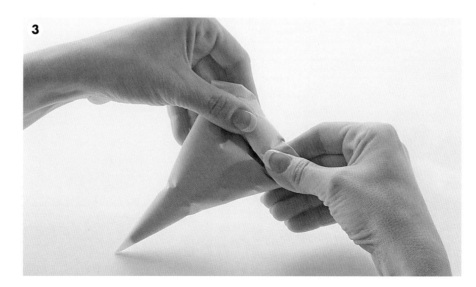

HOLDING THE BAG

Throughout the book, the directions will instruct you to hold the pastry bag at various angles. The most common angles are 45° and 90°. To control the icing, grip the bag with your dominant hand. Use the tip of your index finger of your nondominant hand to guide the bag. Squeeze the icing while guiding the bag.

When positioning a pastry bag at a 45° angle, the bag should be halfway between resting on the surface and standing straight up. A 45° angle is commonly used for piping outlines, filling in outlines, piping leaves, stripes, writing, and figure piping.

The pastry bag is positioned straight up at a 90° angle. This angle is commonly used for piping dots, balls, flowers, and some figure piping.

Prevent Drying

Be sure to keep filled pastry bags covered with a damp cloth or with a tip cover when not in use to avoid hardened or crusted icing.

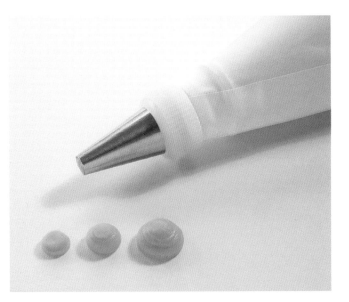

Applying proper pressure is key to successful piping. The amount of pressure may vary depending on what is piped, but in most cases, consistency is important. Shown are piped dots using a #10 tip with small, medium, and large amounts of pressure.

Royal Icing

In cookie decorating, royal icing is typically used for three purposes. The first and most common use is to take the fluffy royal icing and thin it with water to create a glaze called run sugar or flood icing. Adding water to the royal icing creates a sweet, firm icing that dries with a hard finish but will not be difficult to bite into. The second use of royal icing is to pipe outlines and designs for techniques such as brush embroidery or flocking. Third, royal icing is used as a glue when assembling houses, creating stand-up cookies (page 63), and other three-dimensional cookie projects.

The two royal icing recipes in this book both yield a stiff, fluffy icing. A commercial royal icing mix is also available for convenience. Simply add water to the powdered mix and beat on high for several minutes. Mixing bowls and utensils should be spotless and grease free; grease will break down the royal icing and cause the cookies to become spotted. This icing dries out easily, so keep bowls of royal icing and the tips of pastry bags filled with the icing covered with a damp towel. Royal icing mixed from egg whites should be used within the day. Royal icing made with meringue powder or prepared with a commercial royal icing mix can be stored in an airtight container for several days. Refrigerating the icing will extend the shelf life for up to two weeks. The icing consistency will likely change as it sits. Water may evaporate, causing the icing to stiffen further. Royal icing may also separate. For proper consistency, it is important to thoroughly mix royal icing or run sugar just before using. If the icing is too stiff, add a small amount of water. When piping fine details using a tip #2 or smaller, it is best to use fresh (just mixed) royal icing. Any powdered ingredients, including the powdered royal icing mix, should be sifted when mixing.

Royal icing has a subtle sweetness. Flavor can be added for additional taste. Blend the flavoring by hand, adding a small amount at a time until desired taste is obtained. Water- or alcohol-based flavors are best to use when flavoring royal icing. After royal icing is mixed, add the color and/or flavor. If water will be added to the royal icing, do it after adding the color and flavor. If the flavor or color has thinned the royal icing, powdered sugar may be added to thicken it again.

Egg Whites

To eliminate the risk of salmonella, use dried egg whites. Dried egg whites, available at cake decorating supply stores, are reconstituted with a small amount of water.

Royal Icing Recipe-Meringue Powder

- 4 tablespoons (60 mL) meringue powder

- ½ teaspoon (2.5 mL) cream of tartar

- ⅔ cup (160 mL) water

- 8 cups (888 g) powdered sugar, sifted

- 1 tablespoon (15 mL) gum arabic

In a mixing bowl, combine meringue powder, cream of tartar, and water. Beat on high speed until stiff peaks form. In a separate bowl, stir together the powdered sugar and gum arabic. Mix thoroughly and then add to the meringue. Beat on low speed until ingredients are incorporated; then mix on high speed for several minutes until stiff peaks form. Keep icing covered with a damp towel until ready to use.

Yields 4¾ cups (1.2 L)

Royal Icing Recipe—Egg White

- 1 pound (0.45 kg) powdered sugar

- 3 large egg whites at room temperature

- ⅛ teaspoon (.5 mL) cream of tartar

Sift the powdered sugar. Pour the egg whites into a mixing bowl. Mix in the cream of tartar and powdered sugar. After all the ingredients are incorporated, beat on high speed until stiff peaks form. Keep icing covered with a damp towel until ready to use.

Yields 2½ cups (.625 mL)

CONSISTENCY

The following three pictures show how the thickness of royal icing is good for some techniques, while it is too thick or too thin for other techniques. The same tools are used in each picture. A spatula spreads the icing in the far left. The swirl designs are piped using tip #1.5. The hearts are outlined and filled using tip #1.5. The drop flowers are piped using tip #224. Each chapter that uses royal icing will explain how much water to add. When adding water, blend the water by hand to avoid incorporating extra air.

Royal Icing— Thick Consistency (stiff and medium peak)

Use royal icing after it is mixed to a stiff peak for brush embroidery, page 142, or for making piped drop flowers, page 95, ahead of time. A "stiff peak" means the icing holds its shape when standing upright. Royal icing with a stiff peak may be difficult to squeeze from a bag. Piping royal icing with a medium peak is easier on the hands. Use royal icing after it is mixed with a medium peak for dainty piping, eyelet decorating, page 136, and flocking, page 138. Royal icing mixed at a medium peak will be fluffy, but the peak will be soft and curved and will not stand upright. Stiff or medium-peak royal icing is too thick for filling in outlines (shown on the heart). Royal icing with a stiff or medium peak should not flow from the bag without squeezing.

Royal Icing— Medium Consistency

Mix royal icing according to the recipe until stiff peaks form. Once the icing is thick with a stiff peak, add water to achieve medium consistency. Add the water a drop at a time until the icing is the desired consistency. This consistency of royal icing is used for run sugar, page 64. Fine lines and details may become undefined with this consistency. It is too thin to pipe drop flowers. Royal icing with a medium consistency should flow from the bag with light squeezing.

Royal Icing— Thin Consistency

Mix royal icing according to the recipe until stiff peaks form. Add drops of water until the icing is thin and drips off the spatula. This consistency of royal icing is used to fill in textured fondant, page 110. Royal icing with a thin consistency should flow from the bag without squeezing.

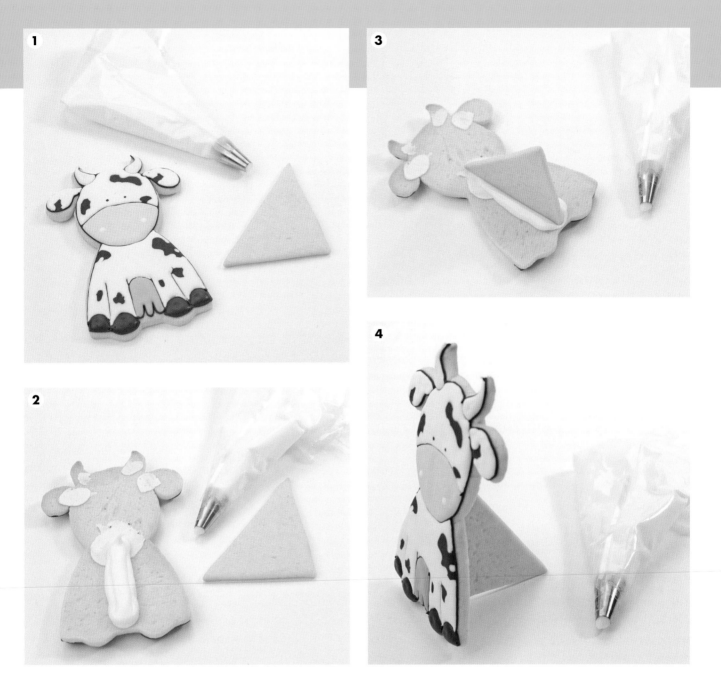

ASSEMBLING THREE-DIMENSIONAL COOKIES USING ROYAL ICING

Nearly any cookie can become a standing cookie with a fitted triangle.

1 Bake and decorate the cookie as desired. Bake and cool a triangle. This will be used to prop the cookie.

2 Fit a bag with tip #10. Fill the bag with royal icing at a stiff peak. Pipe a strip of royal icing on the back of the baked and decorated cookie.

3 Attach the triangle.

4 Stand the cookie. The royal icing should be stiff enough that the cookie can stand up while drying. Keep an eye on the cookie for a few minutes to ensure it does not fall over. If the icing is too thin, the cookie may fall. If it does, add a bit more powdered sugar and try again.

Run Sugar

Run sugar icing is the most commonly used icing for cookies. For years, run sugar–iced cookies have adorned countless magazine covers. Run sugar is created by taking fluffy, stiff royal icing and thinning it to create a glaze, or icing that flows. This icing has a subtle sweetness that is not overpowering. It dries with a matte, hard surface and will have a bit of crunch when bitten. Because this icing dries hard, cookies decorated with it stack and ship well; just allow the cookies to dry several hours or overnight first.

Keep icing bowls covered with a damp cloth to prevent the run sugar from forming a crust. Run sugar in bowls or pastry bags should be fine for a few hours; however the icing thickens as water evaporates. The run sugar may also separate. If it thickens or separates, remove the icing from the bag, stir, and add water if necessary. Keep the tips covered with a damp cloth. When done for the day, squeeze the leftover icing from the bags into bowls. Cover the bowls with an airtight lid for up to a week unrefrigerated or for up to two weeks refrigerated.

Remember, run sugar begins to dry as soon as it hits the air, so when decorating it is important to fill in the outlines quickly.

After the cookies are decorated, keep them on the work surface or place them on a cookie sheet or tray to dry for several hours. Moving the cookies while they are drying may cause tiny cracks to develop on the surface. If the cookies are placed on a tray to dry, use as little movement as possible while moving the tray.

THINNING ROYAL ICING TO CREATE RUN SUGAR

Run sugar is created by adding water to royal icing. Gently fold the water into the icing by hand. Whipping the icing too vigorously or using a mixer will incorporate too much air, causing air bubbles to appear on the decorated cookies. Add enough water to the royal icing so that when piping, the icing will smooth itself in 7–10 seconds. Run sugar should be about the consistency of honey. Each mixed batch of royal icing will vary in viscosity, so the amount of water needed may vary from batch to batch.

Use this icing to outline a cookie, and then immediately fill in the outline to create a decorated cookie without a strong, visible outline. The outline can also be piped and then filled in with a contrasting color of icing. The outline and fill should be the same consistency. Although some decorators prefer to outline the cookie in a stiff icing and fill in the outline with a thinner icing, I prefer to use icings of the same thickness. This makes mixing and cleaning easier, and prevents the icings from bleeding into one another.

Easy Filling

For ease in filling squeeze bottles and pastry bags, use bowls with squared edges or bowls with a spout.

1 Mix royal icing according to recipe directions. The royal icing should be stiff. Add food color if desired.

2 Add a few drops of water to the royal icing. Gently fold the water into the icing. Continue adding drops of water until the royal icing is a honey-like consistency. Spoon a small amount of thinned run sugar onto parchment paper.

3 Drag a knife through the center. The icing should hold its shape, but smooth back together within 7 to 10 seconds. If the icing is too thick, it will remain separated; add more water and repeat the test. If the icing is too thin, it will create a larger puddle and will smooth together quickly; add more icing or powdered sugar to thicken the icing.

4 Once the icing is the proper consistency, spoon it into a pastry bag. A pastry bag holder (shown) is ideal to keep the icing bag upright when filling. A tall drinking glass may also be used. After the bag is filled, fold the corners (see page 55 for pastry bags and parchment cones). If the icing flows from the pastry bag without squeezing, the icing should be thicker.

1

2

3

4

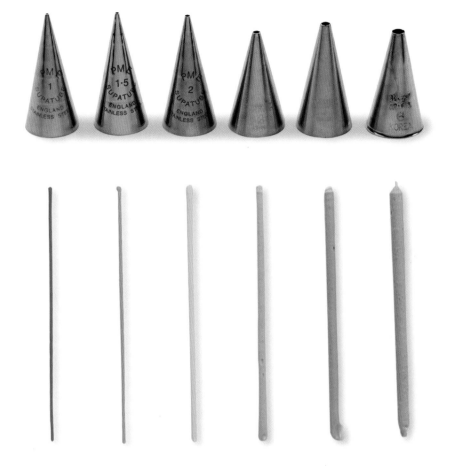

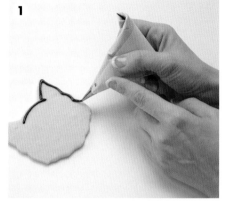

CHOOSING THE RIGHT DECORATING TIP FOR OUTLINING

The cookie size determines which decorating tip to use. Use these guidelines for most decorating. For the most precise outline and fine details, use a decorating tip.

Cookies smaller than 2" (5.1 cm): Tip #1 (red) or #1.5 (orange)

Cookies 2" to 3" (5.1 to 7.6 cm): Tip #1.5 (orange) or 2 (yellow)

Cookies 3" to 4" (7.6 to 10.2 cm): Tip #2 (yellow) or #3 (green)

Cookies 4" to 6" (10.2 to 15.2 cm): Tip #3 (green) or #4 (blue)

VISIBLE OUTLINE WITH RUN SUGAR

1 Fit a pastry bag with a small, round opening such as #1.5 or #2. Fill the bag with run sugar icing. Hold the bag at a 45° angle with your dominant hand. Use your index finger of your nondominant hand to guide the bag. Touch the cookie with the piping tip to attach the icing. After the icing has attached to the cookie, continue squeezing and lift the icing, outlining the cookie. The pastry tip should be slightly raised above the cookie while outlining. Touch the cookie to guide the end of the outline. The tip should touch the cookie to attach the icing and to end the outline. It also may be necessary to touch the cookie when piping sharp corners.

2 Outline any additional areas. Allow the outlines to dry for several minutes.

3

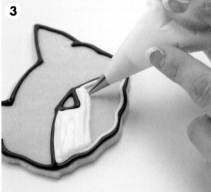

4

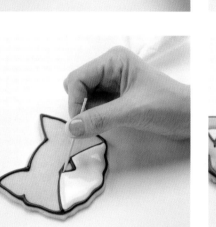

5

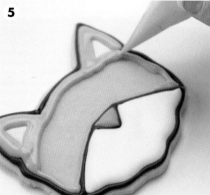

6

- If the icing is not smooth, and the piping lines are visible after filling in the outline, the icing is too thick. The icing may be helped along by resting the iced cookie in the palm of your hand. Tap the back of your palm gently on the work surface to smooth the cookie. If there are still wrinkles, remove the icing from the pastry bag and blend the icing with a few drops of water before decorating the next cookie.

- When filling in an outline, a parchment cone with a hole cut works as well as a tip. This cuts down on your washing. Plus, it's easier to unclog a bag with a cut hole instead of a tip. For smaller cookies, cut the parchment cone to size #3 for filling in outlines, or if using a tip, use tip #3. Tip #4 or #5 is better for filling in outlines on larger cookies. Use the recommended pastry tips for the following techniques.

3 With run sugar in a contrasting color, fill a pastry bag fit with a round opening such as #3 or #4, or cut a hole at the point of a parchment cone. Follow the original outline using the contrasting color of run sugar, piping a second outline inside the first. Fill in the contrasting outline. Do not leave any area uniced, or the icing may come together on its own, trapping air. Trapped air may cause unsightly craters to develop on the iced cookie top.

4 Use a toothpick to spread icing into sharp angles. A toothpick can also be used to remove tiny air bubbles that may have risen to the surface immediately after filling in the outline.

5 Fill in additional colors. Again, use a toothpick to spread icing into sharp angles.

6 If fine details are desired, allow the cookie to dry several hours. Pipe additional details. For fine details, see Detailed Piping with Royal Icing on page 74. Allow the cookie to dry several additional hours or overnight before packaging or stacking the cookies.

NO OUTLINE

1 Fit a pastry bag with a small, round opening such as #1.5 or #2, and fill the bag with run sugar icing. Hold the bag at a 45° angle with your dominant hand. Use your index finger of your nondominant hand to guide the bag. Touch the cookie with the piping tip to attach the icing. After the icing has attached to the cookie, continue squeezing and lift the icing, outlining the cookie. The pastry tip should be slightly raised above the cookie while outlining. Touch the cookie to guide the end of the outline. The tip should only touch the cookie when attaching the icing or ending the outline.

2 Follow the original outline, creating a second outline inside the first.

3 Continue filling in the shape. Do not leave any area uniced, or the icing may come together on its own, trapping air. Trapped air may cause unsightly craters to develop on the iced cookie.

4 Add adjoining colors. Additional colors can be added immediately and the decorations will dry together as one solid piece, or one color may be piped and allowed to set for an hour or two before an adjoining color is added to give the cookie dimension.

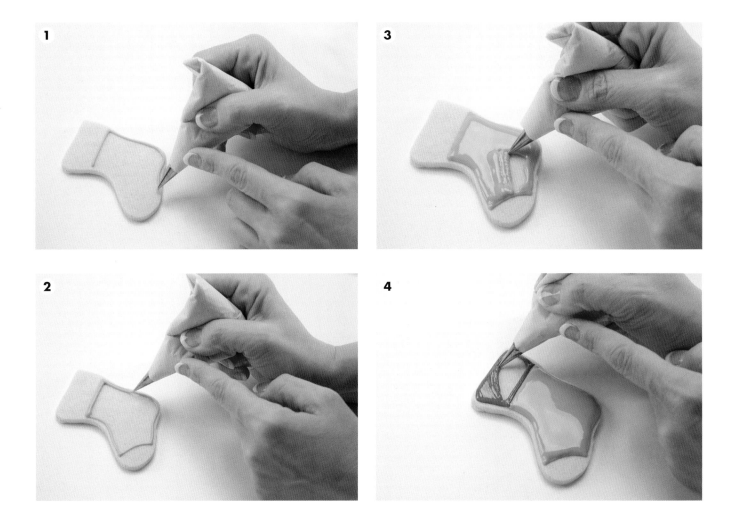

5

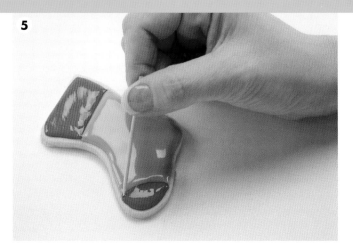

6

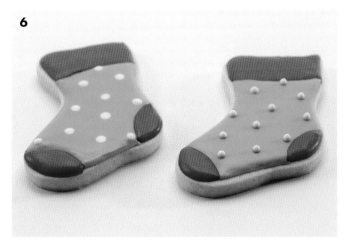

5 Use a toothpick to spread icing into sharp angles. A toothpick can also be used to remove tiny air bubbles that may have risen to the surface immediately after filling in the outline.

6 Details can be added either immediately after outlining and filling or after the icing dries for an hour or two. Details added right away will sink into the icing (dots on the left stocking)—this creates the appearance of one solid, flat piece of icing. Details piped on after an hour or so will add dimension (dots on the right stocking). For more information on adding fine details, see Detailed Piping with Royal Icing on page 74. Allow the cookie to dry several more hours or overnight before packaging or stacking the cookies.

SHADING RUN SUGAR COOKIES

1 Ice the cookies with run sugar following the instructions in the previous sections. Allow the run sugar to completely set.

2 Brush the powder generously onto the area of the cookie that will be shaded. Shown is cosmos petal dust dusted onto the penguin cheeks. Petal dust will provide a matte finish; luster dust a shimmery finish. See pages 39 and 130 for more information on dusting powders.

1

2

STORING RUN SUGAR-ICED COOKIES

The run sugar–decorated cookies can be arranged on a serving plate or placed in cellophane bags after the run sugar has completely dried (allow at least 24 hours).

If the decorated cookies will not be served within a day, place them in an airtight container for up to ten days. The cookies can be stacked in the container, with parchment paper sheets between layers.

Troubleshooting Run Sugar

- Cookies are spotted. Over time, the fats in the cookie may begin to break down the run sugar, which causes unsightly grease spots. Cookie recipes with a high amount of fat, such as a shortbread, may cause grease spots. The recipes in this book are all ideal for run sugar.

- Humidity may also cause spotting. Cookies decorated with run sugar are not best suited for freezing.

- Cracked icing. Moving iced cookies while the run sugar is drying may cause tiny cracks to develop on the cookie surface. Leave cookies on the work surface to dry for several hours. If the cookies are placed on a tray to dry, use as little movement as possible while moving the tray.

- Tiny air bubbles. Tiny air bubbles may surface after the cookie is iced. Use a toothpick to remove any air bubbles before the icing dries. Bubbles may be produced if too much air is incorporated when thinning royal icing to create the run sugar icing. Although a mixer should be used when making royal icing, when transforming it into run sugar icing, blend by hand when adding water. Run sugar that is too thin may contain more air bubbles.

- Small craters. When filling in an outline, do not leave any area uniced, or the icing may come together on its own, trapping air. These trapped air pockets underneath the filled icing may cause the icing to burst with small craters. Craters are more common in small filled areas. Use a toothpick to pop any air pockets before the icing dries.

- Colored streaks in the smooth icing. Streaks are caused by food color that is not thoroughly mixed.

- Bumpy icing. The icing is too thick. Add more water. Taking too much time to fill in the outlined cookie may also cause bumpy icing.

- Icing that is falling off the cookie. The icing is too thin. Thicken with additional royal icing or powdered sugar.

- Puddles. Small water puddles may develop if the icing inside the pastry bag has separated. Run sugar icing in a pastry bag should be good for a couple hours. Icing that will not be used for four hours or more should be removed from the pastry bag or squeeze bottle and placed in an airtight container. Stir the icing before filling a bag.

- Bleeding. When dark or intense colors are next to one another, they may bleed. To avoid this, be sure the two colors of the icings are the same consistency. If bleeding still occurs, allow one color to dry for several hours before adding the adjoining color. Humidity and moisture may also cause the colors to bleed.

- Accent piping is not detailed. Allow each layer to dry before adding any details. Make sure the run sugar is not too thin.

Marbled Run Sugar

Swirls of color create vibrant patterns in cookie icing. The patterns are created by dragging a toothpick through dots or lines in various directions. With this technique, it is important to have all the colors of run sugar in pastry bags ready to go, because cookies iced with run sugar dry quickly. Once the outline is filled, quickly pipe the details or drag the toothpick through, or the icing will begin to set and look uneven. It is also essential that the outline dries before filling in the outline and marbling, or the icing may run off the cookie.

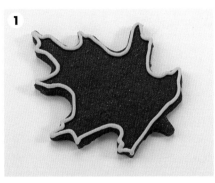

GENERAL INSTRUCTIONS

1 Outline the cookie using a pastry bag fitted with a tip with a small round opening such as #1.5 or #2 and filled with run sugar icing. Hold the bag at a 45° angle with your dominant hand. Use the index finger of your nondominant hand to guide the bag. Touch the cookie with the piping tip to attach the icing. After the icing has attached to the cookie, continue squeezing and lift the icing, outlining the cookie. The pastry tip should be slightly raised above the cookie while outlining. Touch the cookie to guide the end of the outline. The tip should only touch the cookie when attaching or ending the outline. Allow the outline to harden for an hour or two before continuing to step 2.

2 Fill a pastry bag with run sugar in the background color. Fill additional pastry bags with contrasting colors of run sugar and set aside. Using the background color and following the original outline, create a second outline inside the first. Continue filling in the shape. Do not leave any area uniced, or the icing may come together on its own, trapping air. Trapped air may cause unsightly craters to develop on the iced cookie.

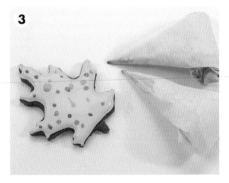

3 Using contrasting colors of icing, pipe dots onto the wet icing.

4 Hold a toothpick at a 90° angle and drag through the run sugar icing in various directions. If the icing begins to build on the toothpick, lift the toothpick, wipe clean, and continue until the desired effect is achieved. Rest the marbled cookie in the palm of your hand. Tap the back of your palm gently on the work surface to smooth the cookie. Allow the cookie to dry several hours or overnight before packaging or stacking the cookies.

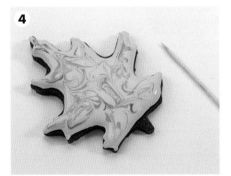

STYLIZED MARBLED DESIGNS

Stripes

Follow steps 1 and 2 for Marbled Run Sugar, page 71. Pipe contrasting rows of stripes. Hold a toothpick at a 90° angle and drag through the run sugar icing in one direction. Lift the toothpick and clean the end. Then drag the toothpick the opposite direction.

Hearts

Follow steps 1 and 2 for Marbled Run Sugar, page 71. Pipe dots. Position the toothpick at the top of the dot. Drag the toothpick down the middle of the dot. Lift toothpick. Always clean the toothpick after lifting and before dragging the toothpick through the icing again.

Fire

Follow steps 1 and 2 for Marbled Run Sugar, page 71. Pipe uneven zigzags starting with yellow at the bottom, orange in the middle, and red at the top. Position the toothpick at the bottom of the yellow zigzag. Drag the toothpick through the yellow and red zigzags. Slightly curve the edge until achieving the desired length. Lift toothpick. Clean the end of the toothpick. Repeat dragging the toothpick through the zigzags, creating different lengths.

Tie-dye

Follow steps 1 and 2 for Marbled Run Sugar, page 71. Pipe a swirl in the center of the cookie (shown in pink). Pipe another color, starting at the end of the first swirl, creating a second swirl. Continue making swirls in various colors. Position the toothpick in the center of the smallest swirl. Drag the toothpick through the swirls and through the adjoining color. Always clean the toothpick after lifting and before dragging the toothpick through the icing again. Repeat dragging the toothpick through the swirls, creating different lengths of stripes.

Detailed Piping with Royal Icing

Piping royal icing onto a cookie using fine piping tips creates beautiful, elegant cookies with delicate details. Detailed piping includes dots, swirls, lines, or lettering. Details can be piped onto rolled fondant–covered cookies, run sugar–iced cookies, or egg wash–glazed cookies. Royal icing should not be piped onto buttercream-iced cookies. The fat in the buttercream icing will cause the royal icing to break down and spot. If the details are piped onto a cookie iced with run sugar, the iced cookie must be completely set or the details will sink into the icing and spread.

The consistency of royal icing is very important for dainty piping. For most piping, the royal icing should be thick and fairly stiff with a medium peak. If the icing is too stiff, it may be difficult to squeeze the bag. If too thin, the piping may blend together and become flat and undefined. The icing should not flow from the pastry bag unless the bag is gently squeezed. Icing can be a tad thinner when piping dots. It is also important to thoroughly sift powdered ingredients before mixing royal icing. Even the tiniest clumps of powdered ingredients may clog the tip. A tip clogged with royal icing may either not release from the tip or it may release with messy bursts of icing. PME tip numbers do not perfectly correspond with American tip numbers, but they are very close. It is handy to keep PME tips #0, #1, #1.5, #2, and #2.5 for dainty piping. Use tip #0 for mini-cookies. Tips #1 and #1.5 are nice for detailing 2" to 4" (5.1 to 10.2 cm) cookies. Use tips #2 or #2.5 for larger cookies. Do not get discouraged if your decorated cookies do not look perfect. It takes practice to master the flow, pressure, and consistency of the icing. The template included in this chapter can be used to practice.

GENERAL DIRECTIONS

1 Ice the cookie with run sugar icing, or cover the cookie with rolled fondant. If the cookie is iced with run sugar, allow the icing to harden several hours. Fit a pastry bag with a small round opening tip, such as #1 or #1.5, and fill the pastry bag with royal icing at medium peak. Touch the iced cookie and squeeze to attach the icing.

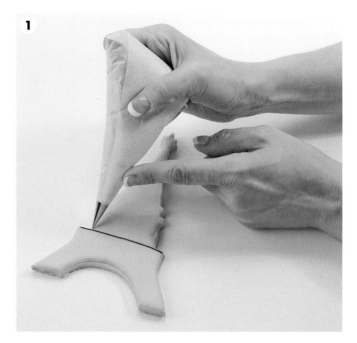

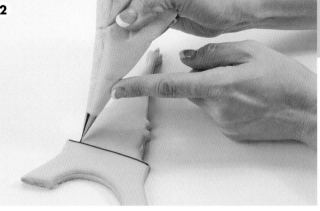

2 While still squeezing, lift the pastry bag and begin piping the details. Continue with steady pressure. Touch the surface and stop squeezing to attach the end of the detail.

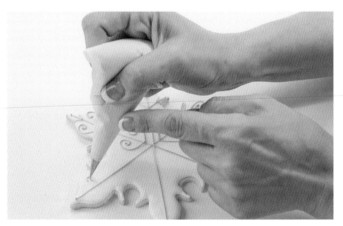

Straight Lines

Hold the pastry bag at a 45° angle. Touch the cookie and gently squeeze the bag to attach the icing. Continue squeezing the bag and lift the bag slightly above the cookie while moving the bag to create a line. When the line is the desired length, touch the cookie to attach the line. To achieve a straight line, steadily move across the cookie with consistent timing and pressure.

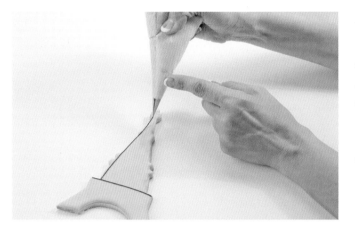

Swirls

Hold the pastry bag at a 45° angle. Touch the cookie and gently squeeze the bag to attach the icing. Continue squeezing the bag and lift the bag slightly above the cookie while moving the bag in the shape of a swirl. When the swirl is complete, touch the cookie to attach the end of the swirl.

Dots

Add a little more water to the royal icing until the consistency becomes medium to thick—thinner than the royal icing just mixed but slightly thicker than icing used for run sugar iced cookies. If too much water is added, the dot will not have much dimension. If too little water is added, there will be peaks on the dots. If the dot has small peaks, dampen your index finger with water and gently press the peak. A small burst of pressure is applied to release icing. Stop pressure, then lift. For very tiny dots, minimal pressure is needed.

Following Texture Lines

Rolled fondant that has been textured, page 106, provides a pattern for piping. If either side of the texture mat can be used, use the side that will provide a raised design. It is easier to pipe on raised lines than in recessed lines.

Practice

Practice piping using the template opposite. Copy or trace the template on a sheet of paper. Place a piece of acetate or transparent parchment paper on top of the template. Practice piping on the acetate or parchment paper. Remember: Do not drag the tip on the surface. The tip should be lifted just abouve.

Wiggly Lines

If your royal icing lines are wiggly, you are applying too much pressure while squeezing the bag or are piping the details too slowly. If the royal icing lines are breaking, you're not applying enough pressure while squeezing the bag. Try to use a gentle amount of consistent pressure while moving your hand across the cookie. Clogged tips may also cause wiggly lines.

Clogged Tips

It's very frustrating to decorate with tips that become clogged. Poke a straight pin into a clogged tip to break the piece causing the clog. (Take care when using a straight pin, or the pin may damage the tip opening.) If the icing continues to clog, remove and clean the tip. Reduce clogs by always sifting any powdered icing ingredients when mixing icing.

Painted Cookies

A white run sugar–iced cookie or white rolled fondant–covered cookie provides the perfect canvas to create edible, painted works of art. Although painting details may sound difficult, it is actually quite easy as cookie cutters provide a nice outline and guide to begin painting. Food color markers or food color thinned with water provide the coloring. Each creates a unique look.

Comparing the two color mediums is like comparing watercolor paints with coloring markers. Food color thinned with water will give a more artistic appearance, while the markers provide a vivid, strong contrast with little shading. Food color gels are ideal for painting on cookies. Adding various amounts of water to the food color gel can create many shades. Liquid food colors do not provide enough concentration to create strong contrasts. Food color markers are ideal for children to use. The markers are handy for outlining or drawing fine details. Food color markers are available from several companies. Americolor has markers in bright vivid colors, while Foodoodler offers several sizes of tip openings.

PAINTING COOKIES

1 Cover the cookie with white rolled fondant following instructions on page 104, or ice a cookie with white run sugar following instructions of page 64. Allow the cookies to crust for 24 hours before painting. Fill each cavity of a paint tray half full of water. Squirt small amounts of food color gel onto the top of a clean paint tray. Blend some of the food color gel with the water in the cavities until the desired shade is achieved. Test the color on a white sheet of paper.

Painting Pointers

Make sure the brush is damp with the food color paint and not dripping with water. Too much water on the brush will cause the sugars to dissolve in the rolled fondant or run sugar icing. This will produce dark spotting or tiny air bubbles. Tiny air bubbles may also appear if the cookie was covered with run sugar that was too thin.

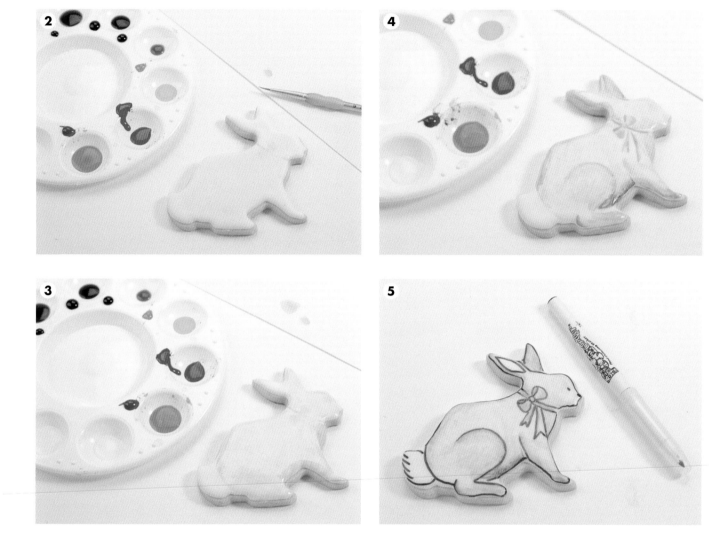

2 Paint any details with a very light shade of the color desired.

3 Paint around the details. Leave a thin white line between adjoining colors to prevent bleeding. Decide which areas will remain white, and outline with the color that will surround the white area. For example, the bunny will be painted pink, but the inside of his ear will remain white.

4 Blend the concentrated food color on the top of the paint tray with a small amount of water to create a thick, dark paint for shading. Test the color on a white sheet of paper. Use the shading color to add contrast and shading to the cookie.

5 Allow the painted cookie to dry for several hours. Outline the cookie using a fine brush with concentrated food color, or use fine-tip food color markers.

FOOD COLOR MARKERS

1 Cover the cookie with white rolled fondant following the instructions on page 104, or ice a cookie with white run sugar following the instructions of page 64. Allow the cookies to dry for 24 hours before coloring.

2 Color the details using the food color markers.

3 Color around the details. Leave a thin white line between adjoining colors to prevent bleeding.

4 Outline the colors using a fine-tip black food color marker.

Create a watercolor effect by coloring the cookie with a marker, then using a brush dampened with water to blend the food color with a small amount of water.

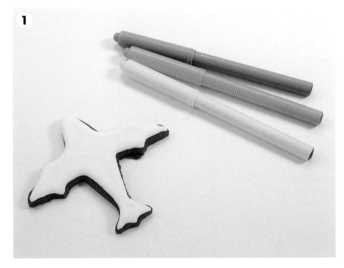

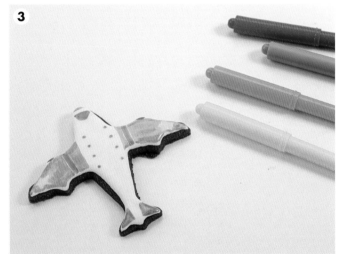

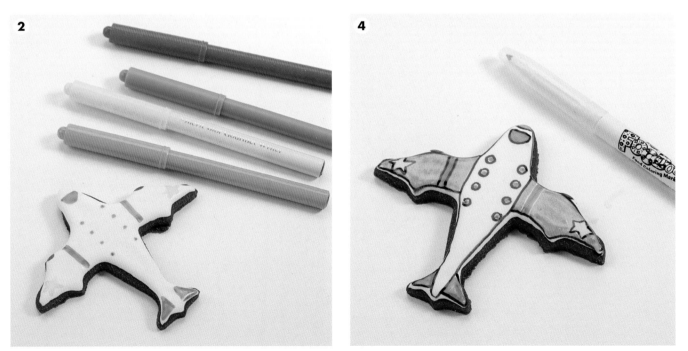

Dry First

Be sure to allow the rolled fondant to dry for several hours or overnight, or the marker will indent the fondant when coloring. Also allow the run sugar to dry for several hours or overnight, or the markers will poke through the icing

STORING PAINTED RUN SUGAR-ICED COOKIES

The run sugar painted cookies can be arranged on a serving plate or placed in cellophane bags after the painting has completely dried (allow at least 6 hours). If the food color was not thinned with water, the painted cookie may remain sticky and leave residue in the cellophane bags.

If the decorated cookies will not be served within a day, place them in an airtight container for up to ten days. The cookies can be stacked in the container, with parchment paper between each layer.

Buttercream Icing

There is no other icing like buttercream. It is a sweet, fluffy icing that can be spread onto cookies or piped using various tips. Piping with buttercream is fun for kids. Children love to see all the unique textures that are possible while squeezing the delicious icing.

Buttercream can be made by following this recipe or it can be purchased premade from cake and candy supply stores. Although the icing will form a crust when it dries, it will remain soft and creamy on the inside. The icing may not crust in geographical areas that are humid. Colored buttercream may darken as the color sets, especially with deep colors such as red, emerald green, navy, purple, or black. Blend the color a shade lighter than the desired color. Wait for a few hours, and then check. If the icing is too light, add more food coloring. If the icing is too dark, add more white buttercream. When piping icing onto the cookies, start with extra-thick cookies or the sweetness from the icing will overpower the cookie. If the icing will be spread onto the cookie, the cookie does not need to be as thick. Buttercream is a basic, sweet icing that can be modified with a variety of flavors. Substitute the almond flavor with any extract. Popular extracts are peppermint, lemon, coconut, and coffee. Extracts and flavorings will vary in potency. Add to taste. Some flavors contain color that may affect the tinge of the icing.

Buttercream Icing Recipe

- ½ cup (120 mL) high-ratio shortening
- 4 cups (520 g) powdered sugar, sifted
- 5 tablespoons (75 mL) water
- ½ teaspoon (2.5 mL) salt
- 1 teaspoon (5 mL) vanilla flavoring
- ½ teaspoon (2.5 mL) almond flavoring
- ¼ teaspoon (1.5 mL) butter flavoring

In a large bowl, combine ingredients; beat on low speed until well blended. Continue beating on low speed for 10 minutes or until very creamy. Keep the bowl covered to prevent the icing from drying out. Unused icing can be kept in the refrigerator up to six weeks. Rewhip on low speed before piping.

Yields 4 cups (1 L)

SPREADING THE ICING

1 Scoop a generous amount of buttercream icing onto the baked and cooled cookie.

2 Spread the icing to apply an even thickness. It is okay if some of the icing extends beyond the edge of the cookie.

3 Take a clean spatula with a thin blade and scrape along the edge of the cookie, holding the spatula at a 90° angle.

4 Allow the icing to crust. Gently roll over the iced cookie with a pastry roller to smooth any rough areas.

1

2

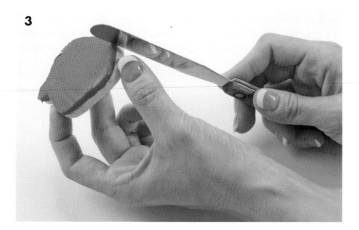

3

4

- For bright white icing, use clear flavorings. Pure vanilla will give the icing an ivory hue.

- Solid vegetable shortening can be substituted for high-ratio shortening. High-ratio shortening is a shortening produced to replace butter. It is a baker's quality shortening and is used in icing and cake recipes. High-ratio shortening gives the icing a fine, smooth, and creamy texture without a greasy aftertaste. It is likely that solid vegetable shortening may affect the icing consistency, texture, and flavor.

- Do not whip the icing on medium or high speed. Extra air will be incorporated causing air bubbles. Whipping the buttercream on low speed creates a smooth and creamy icing.

- Food color in buttercream icing may deepen upon setting. Allow the icing to set for two to three hours to see true color.

- A delicious chocolate buttercream icing can be made with the simple addition of cocoa powder. Add approximately 1 cup (125 g) of cocoa powder to the buttercream recipe. Be aware that the cocoa powder may cause the buttercream to stiffen; add a small amount of water to achieve the desired consistency.

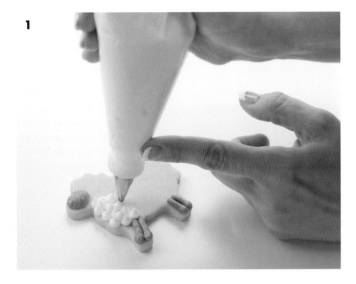

1

PIPING DOTS

1 Fit a pastry bag with a round opening tip. Hold the pastry bag at a 90° angle just above the cookie.

2 Squeeze the bag and apply pressure to pipe a dot, holding the tip steady to allow the icing to form around the tip. Continue squeezing until the dot is the desired size. Stop squeezing; then lift bag.

3 If the dot has a peak, use your index finger to gently flatten before the icing forms a crust.

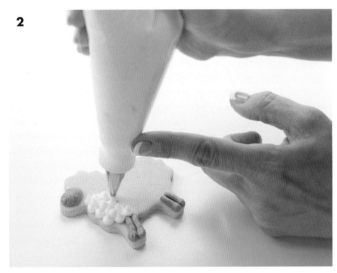

2

3

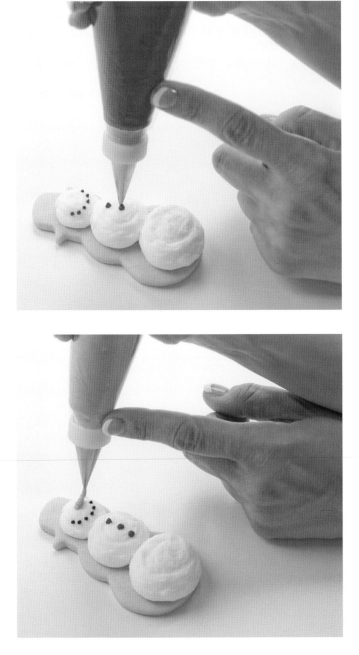

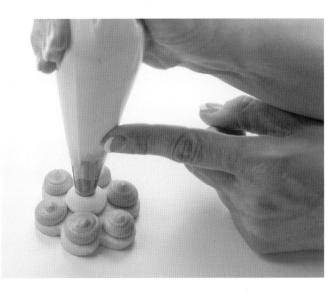

Tip #2A

#2A is used to pipe simple flower petals and the flower center.

A 4" (10.2 cm) tall snowman is made by piping several dots in various sizes for all the details. Each snowball is piped using tip #1A. The larger the snowball, the more pressure was applied. The buttons on the middle snowball are piped using tip #3. The snowman's eyes and mouth are piped using tip #1. His carrot nose is piped using tip #2 with a lot of pressure while pulling up the icing.

1 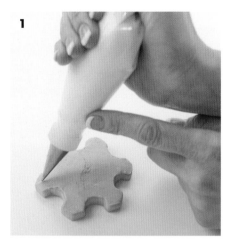 **2**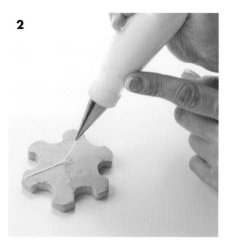

PIPING LINES

1 Fit a pastry bag with a round opening tip. Position the pastry bag at a 45° angle. Touch the cookie. Squeeze the pastry bag to release icing; then lift icing just above the cookie, continuing with pressure.

2 Squeeze the bag and continually apply pressure while moving your hand across the cookie. Let the icing flow from the bag naturally above the surface. Do not drag the tip on the cookie. Stop pressure. Touch the cookie to attach the end of the line and lift the pastry bag.

Perfect Lines

If the lines are wiggly, you may be applying too much pressure. If the lines are breaking, either you are not applying enough pressure or the piping bag is moving too fast.

1 **2**

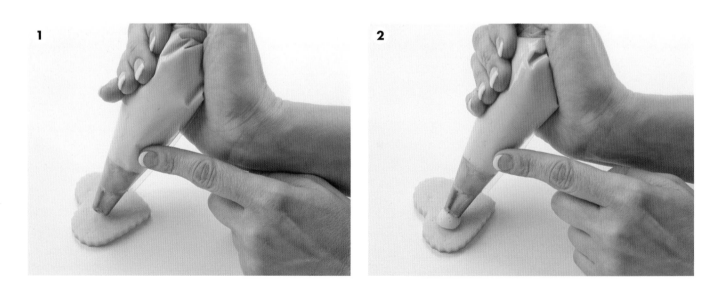

TEARDROPS

1 Fit a pastry bag with a round opening tip. Position the pastry bag at a 45° angle with the tip nearly touching the cookie.

2 Squeeze the bag and apply pressure to form a teardrop, beginning at the thick end.

3

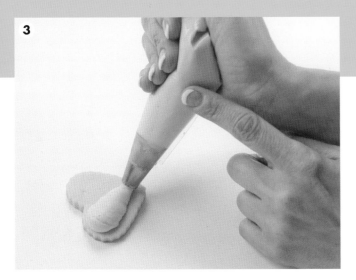

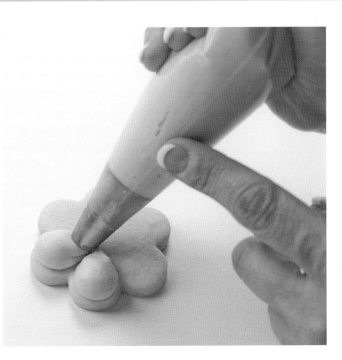

3 Gradually release pressure and drag the tip to form the narrow end of the teardrop. Stop pressure and lift the pastry bag.

Piped teardrops make great petals for retro flowers.

A heart is made by piping two teardrops.

1

2

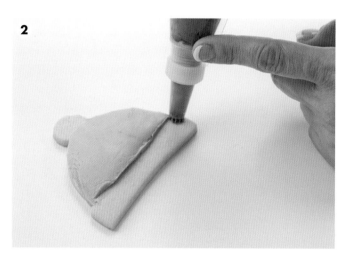

3

PIPING FUR, GRASS, OR FINE BRANCHES

1 Fit a pastry bag with tip #233. Position the pastry bag at a 90° angle with the tip touching the cookie.

2 Squeeze the bag and apply pressure to attach the icing.

Angles

Hold the bag at a 90 ° angle to produce fur or grass that is standing straight up. Hold the tip at a 45° angle to produce fur or grass that lies somewhat flat.

4

3 Continue with pressure and pull the icing. Stop pressure and lift the pastry bag.

4 Continue piping the fur, grass, or fine branches, piping close together.

1

2

3

4

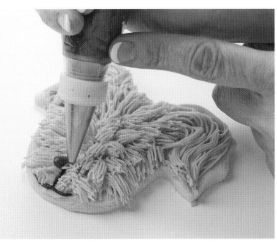

5

3 Pipe the next row and allow the fur to fall over the top of the first row. Continue with rows of fur, working toward the center.

5 Details such as the puppy's eyes and nose are piped after the fur is completely added so they stand out.

(continued)

1 Applying generous pressure while continuously moving along the cookie will produce long strands of fur.

2 Details such as the puppy's mouth may be piped first. This allows the fur to fall around the details.

3 When piping, pipe the fur strands side by side in a row.

1. To pipe branches on a Christmas tree, start at the bottom of the tree and pipe a row of long strands.

2. Start a second row of branches just above the first row.

3. Continue piping, starting each row just above the preceding until the tree is full.

1

3

2

4

PIPING WITH LEAF TIPS

1 Fit a pastry bag with a leaf opening tip such as #352.
Position the pastry bag at a 45° angle. One of the points
should be touching the cookie. The other point should be
parallel with the point touching the cookie.

2 Squeeze the bag and apply pressure to attach the icing.

3 Continue with pressure and pull the icing to form a leaf.
Stop pressure and remove the pastry bag.

4 Continue piping leaves, starting each row just above the
preceding row until the tree is full.

(continued)

To pipe a longer leaf, apply generous pressure while moving your hand until the leaf is the desired length.

A poinsettia is piped using leaf tip #352 for the green leaves and red petals. The background green leaves are piped first, followed by a layer of red petals. The final layer of red petals are made using the same tip, but applying less pressure for the smaller petals. The center is piped using tip #2 and yellow and green icing.

STAR TIP

1 Fit a pastry bag with a star opening tip such as #32. Hold the pastry bag at a 90° angle just above the cookie.

2 Squeeze the bag and apply pressure to pipe a star, holding the tip steady to allow the icing to form around the tip.

3 Continue squeezing until the star is the desired size. Stop squeezing; then lift bag. Allow the star to crust. If the star has peaks, use your index finger to gently flatten them.

Use a small star tip, such as #16, to pipe textured lines, or wiggle the tip while squeezing to create a zigzag pattern.

BASKETWEAVE

1 Fit a pastry bag with a bas-keketweave opening tip, such as #46. Position the pastry bag at a 45° angle, touching the cookie. Squeeze the bag and apply pressure. Pipe a vertical line the height of the area covered.

2 Pipe short, horizontal lines over the vertical line, allowing a space the width of the tip between each horizontal line.

3 Cover the ends of the horizontal line with another vertical line.

4 Start the next group of horizontal lines in the empty space, holding the tip against the first vertical line. Cross over the second vertical line.

5 Repeat, piping vertical and horizontal lines until the cookie is finished.

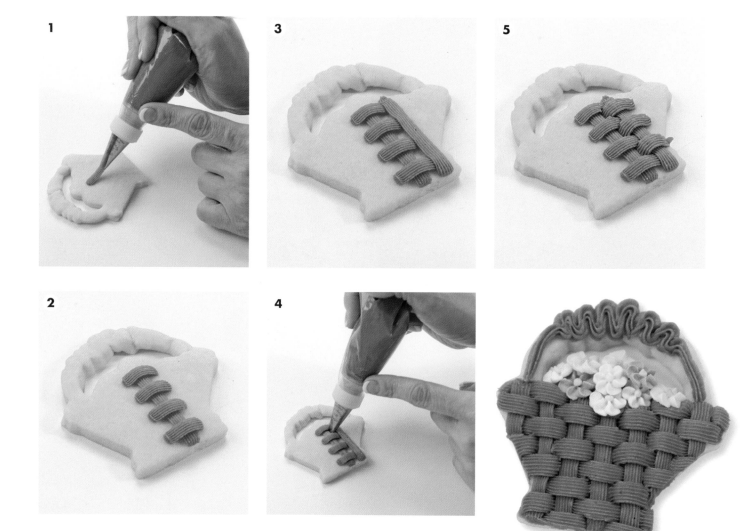

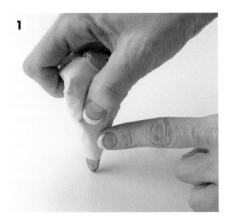

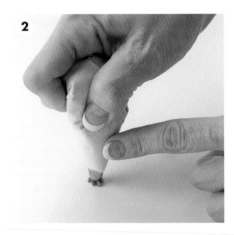

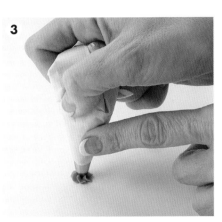

For the most defined petals, apply pressure and turn at the same time. Do not apply pressure without turning, or turn without applying pressure.

DROP FLOWERS

1 Fit a pastry bag with a drop flower tip, such as #224, and fill with stiff royal icing or buttercream icing. Place a sheet of parchment paper on the work surface; secure the paper to the work surface with a couple dots of icing. Start with the pastry bag at a 90° angle, touching the surface.

2 Apply pressure while turning the tip a quarter turn, keeping the tip touching the surface.

3 Continue with pressure while turning. Release pressure and raise the tip straight up with a slight jerk to break off the icing.

4 Use a contrasting color and pipe a dot in the center.

5 For buttercream flowers, slide the parchment paper onto a cookie sheet and place flowers in the freezer to harden. Remove one flower at a time and place the cold flower on the cookie. For royal icing flowers, allow several hours or overnight for the flowers to dry completely at room temperature. When dry, place in an airtight container. Royal icing flowers will last for several months.

1

4

2

3

BOWS

1 Fit a pastry bag with a nongrooved basketweave tip, such as tip #44. Position the pastry bag at a 45° angle, touching the cookie. Squeeze the bag and apply pressure. Pipe a vertical line for the ribbon strands.

2 If the ribbon has angled points, hold the spatula perpendicular to the cookie and scrape excess icing. This will form points in the icing.

3 Position the pastry bag at a 45° angle, touching the cookie. Squeeze the bag and apply pressure. Pipe a backward C for the ribbon loop, returning to the center.

4 Repeat with the second loop, piping another C. Using the same nongrooved basketweave tip, pipe an oval for the center of the bow.

PIPING WITH ROUND OPENINGS

Use various amounts of pressure and movements to figure pipe onto cookies while continuing to squeeze until the desired effect is achieved.

For the lamb legs, continuous pressure is applied; then a burst of pressure is used to pipe the feet.

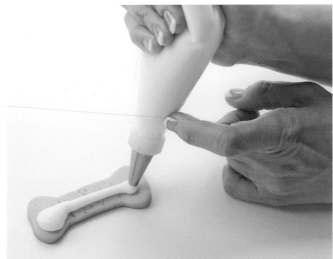

To pipe a bone, first pipe a teardrop and then apply continuous pressure while piping a line and then a final teardrop.

(continued)

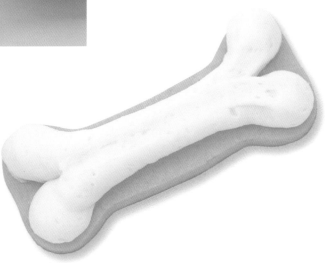

Use a large round tip opening, such as tip #1A, to pipe various sizes of teardrops. The duck's head is piped first.

With the same tip that was used for the head and the body, pipe a wing using very little pressure.

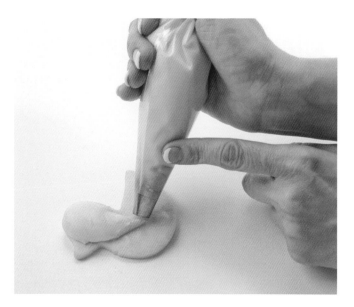

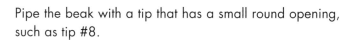

With the same tip that was used for the duck's head, apply a second teardrop for the body. Apply more pressure to make a larger teardrop.

Pipe the beak with a tip that has a small round opening, such as tip #8.

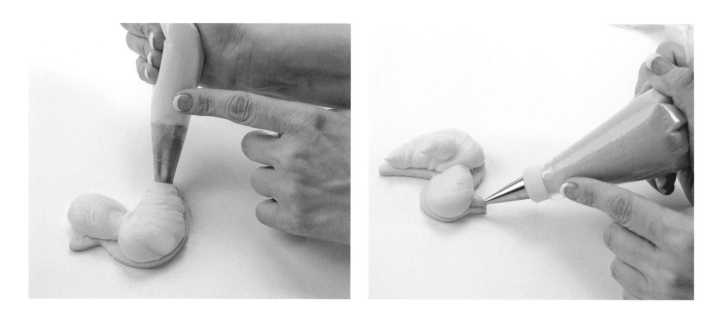

STORING BUTTERCREAM ICED COOKIES

Cookies iced with buttercream should be eaten within seven days. They are best kept at room temperature. Buttercream icing on the cookies should form a crust, which allows the cookies to be gently stacked on a serving plate or placed in individual cellophane bags. Buttercream icing may not crust in geographical areas where it is very humid, or if the iced cookies have been kept in the refrigerator or freezer.

If the iced cookies will not be served within a day, store them in a single layer in a loosely covered container. If the container is tightly closed or if the container is placed in the refrigerator or freezer, condensation may form. Condensation may cause spots or colors to bleed.

Buttercream-decorated cookies are not ideal for shipping: the icing will likely be smashed in the process with all details lost; plus heat may cause the icing to melt.

Rolled Fondant

Rolled fondant is an icing that is rolled, cut, and placed on the cookie to create a smooth, clean finish. It is similar to working with clay or sculpting dough. Rolled fondant can be sculpted, cut, or textured. It is commonly used as a sweet decorative covering on a cake. In the United States, most people prefer the flavor of buttercream on cake. The chewy, sweet rolled fondant covering can be rather heavy and in stark contrast to the texture of the soft, moist cake that is typically served in the United States. However, rolled fondant serves as a wonderful sweet complement to cutout cookies.

The rolled fondant should be about half as thick as the baked cookie or the rolled fondant will overpower the cookie. A recipe is included for those who wish to make rolled fondant from scratch. However, it can be time consuming and difficult to make. Before attempting the recipe, purchase commercial rolled fondant to become familiar with the proper texture. Commercial rolled fondant varies in texture and flavor, and is available in white or colors. If rolled fondant is overworked or if it seems dry, it will be stiff and tough on the cookie. A touch of shortening or egg whites can be added to soften the fondant. See page 152 for information about creating accents and details using rolled fondant on cookies. These accents can be added to nearly any type of cookie icing.

Rolled Fondant Recipe

- ½ cup (120 g) cream
- 2 tablespoons (30 mL) unflavored gelatin
- ¾ cup (175 mL) glucose
- 2 tablespoons (28 g) butter
- 2 tablespoons (25 mL) glycerin
- 2 teaspoons (10 mL) clear vanilla flavor
- 2 teaspoons (10 mL) clear butter flavor
- 1 teaspoon (5 mL) almond flavor
- approximately 9 cups (1 kg) powdered sugar

Pour cream into a small saucepan. Sprinkle gelatin on cream and cook on low until the gelatin dissolves. Add glucose, butter, glycerin, and flavorings. Heat until butter is melted. Set aside. Sift the powdered sugar. Place 7 cups (770 g) of powdered sugar in a mixer bowl. Pour the cream mixture over the powdered sugar, and mix slowly with a dough hook until thoroughly combined. Add the additional 2 cups (220 g) of powdered sugar. The fondant will be very sticky but should hold its shape. Lay a sheet of plastic wrap on the counter, and coat with a thin layer of vegetable shortening. Wrap the fondant in the greased plastic wrap and allow to set for 24 hours. After 24 hours, the fondant should be less sticky. If the fondant is still sticky, add more powdered sugar.

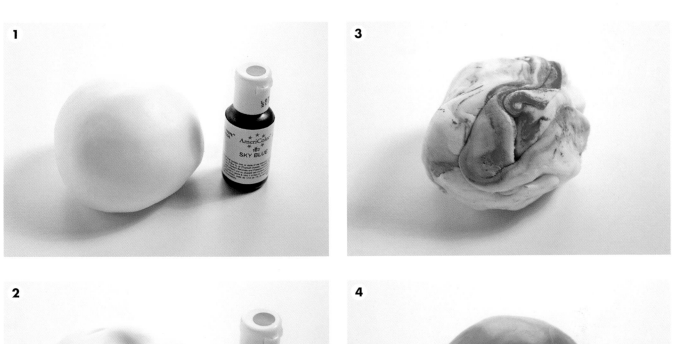

COLORING ROLLED FONDANT

1 Start with kneaded and soft rolled fondant.

2 Add color to the fondant by using a toothpick for color in jars or squeezing the color onto the fondant if the color is in tubes.

3 Begin kneading the color into the fondant. Add more color, if desired, to darken.

4 Knead thoroughly until there are no streaks of color.

Color Mixing Tips

- Rub a small amount of shortening into your hands before kneading color into the fondant to prevent bad stains on your hands. Food service plastic gloves can also be worn to keep hands stain-free.

- Color a little more fondant than you think you'll need. It is difficult to duplicate the exact shade if you run out.

MARBELIZING ROLLED FONDANT—METHOD ONE

1 Start with soft and pliable rolled fondant. Add color to the fondant by using a toothpick for color in jars or squeezing the color onto the fondant if the color is in tubes.

2 Knead fondant only slightly so streaks remain.

3 Roll the fondant and cut designs.

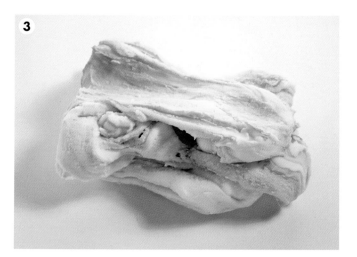

MARBELIZING ROLLED FONDANT—METHOD TWO

1 Knead and soften each color of rolled fondant. The lighter color should be two-thirds larger than the darker color.

2 Place ropes of colored fondant side by side.

3 Fold the fondant. Begin kneading and folding to create marbleized streaks.

4 Roll the fondant and cut designs.

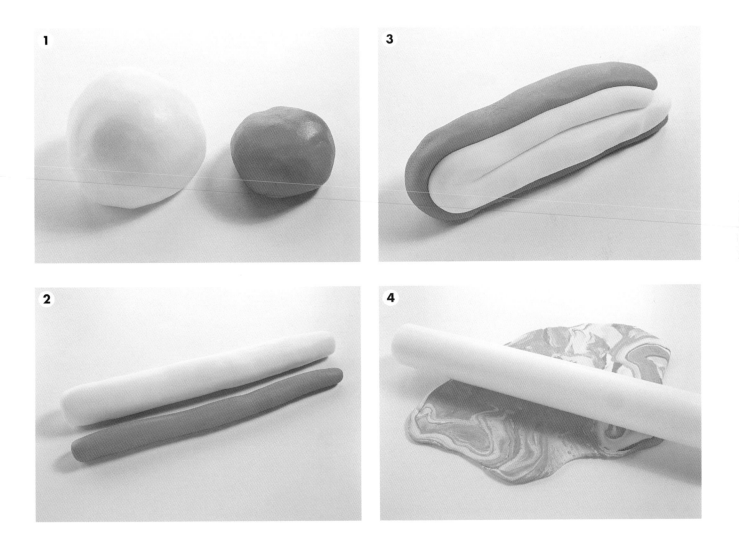

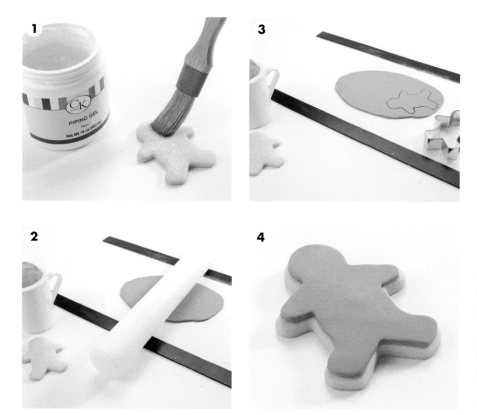

Buttercream icing can be used in place of piping gel for additional sweetness. Pipe buttercream icing on the cookie using tip #6, leaving approximately ½" (1.3 cm) uniced along the outer edges of the cookie. Use a spatula with a thin blade to smooth the buttercream, taking care not to spread the icing off the cookie. Place the rolled fondant on top of the buttercream-iced cookie.

COVERING A COOKIE WITH ROLLED FONDANT

1 Brush a thin layer of piping gel on a baked and cooled cookie. A few cookies may be brushed at a time with the piping gel, but take note that the gel dries fairly quickly.

2 Knead and soften the rolled fondant. Lightly dust the work surface with powdered sugar to create a nonstick surface. Place the rolled fondant on the dusted surface between two perfection strips, 2 mm thick. Roll over the strips, thinning the rolled fondant. Rolled fondant is rolled between perfection strips to give a perfect thickness, or use a rolling pin with rings. When rolling, lift and turn the rolled fondant a quarter turn. Do not turn the rolled fondant over. If the rolled fondant is sticking while lifting and turning, dust with additional powdered sugar or knead powdered sugar into the rolled fondant to stiffen. Keep the top of the rolled fondant free of powdered sugar, or the covered cookie will have white spots or a white powdery finish.

3 Cut the rolled fondant with the same cutter that was used for the cookie.

4 Lift the shape and place on the cookie brushed with piping gel.

PIECED ROLLED FONDANT COOKIES

1 Follow steps 1 to 3 for Covering a Cookie with Rolled Fondant.

2 Using a mini–pizza cutter, cut any area that should be a different color. Use a paring knife to cut small areas.

3 Place the cut piece on the cookie brushed with piping gel.

4 With a contrasting color of rolled fondant, follow steps 1 to 3 for Covering a Cookie with Rolled Fondant. Cut the remaining area.

5 Place the cut fondant on the cookie and piece together.

COVERING A COOKIE WITH TEXTURED ROLLED FONDANT

1 Brush a thin layer of piping gel on a baked and cooled cookie. A few cookies may be brushed at a time with the piping gel, but take note that the gel dries fairly quickly. Knead and soften the rolled fondant. Lightly dust the work surface with powdered sugar to create a nonstick surface. Place the rolled fondant on the dusted surface between two perfection strips, 2 mm thick. Roll over the strips, thinning the rolled fondant. The rolled fondant is rolled between perfection strips to give a perfect thickness, or use a rolling pin with rings. When rolling, lift and turn the rolled fondant a quarter turn. Do not turn the rolled fondant over. If the rolled fondant is sticking while lifting and turning, dust with additional powdered sugar or knead powdered sugar into the rolled fondant to stiffen. Keep the top of the rolled fondant free of powdered sugar, or the covered cookie will have white spots or a white powdery finish.

2 Remove the perfection strips. Place a texture mat on the work surface. Many texture mats are double sided. Either side may be used. One side will give a recessed impression, and one will give a raised impression. Place the smooth, rolled side of the fondant facedown on the texture mat. Start on the end of the texture mat and roll over the rolled fondant with a generous amount of pressure.

3 Flip the texture mat with the rolled fondant over. Peel back the mat.

4 Cut the rolled fondant with the same cutter that was used for the cookie.

5 Lift the shape and place on the cookie brushed with piping gel.

A textured cookie with contrasting colors or textures can be made by combining these instructions with the instructions for Pieced Rolled Fondant Cookies. If combining a textured section with a nontexture section, such as the pink and yellow egg, the pieces look nicer if they are the same thickness. Both the pink and yellow pieces are rolled between 2 mm perfection strips. The strips are removed, and the pink is rolled over the texture mat, which makes the piece thinner than 2 mm. After the yellow is rolled between perfection strips, remove the strips and roll over the rolled fondant one more time to achieve the same thickness as the pink.

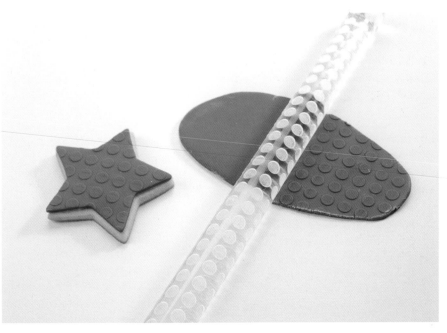

Fondant Sticking

If the rolled fondant is sticking to the texture mat or textured rolling pin, knead additional powdered sugar into the rolled fondant. The texture mat or rolling pin can also be lightly coated with a cooking spray. Remove excess spray with a paper towel. Use the cooking spray only if necessary. If too much spray is used, the details will not be as sharp.

There are also texture rolling pins you can use. Follow steps 1 to 2 for Covering a Cookie with Rolled Fondant. Remove the perfection strips. Starting at one end of the rolled fondant, roll over the fondant with generous pressure.

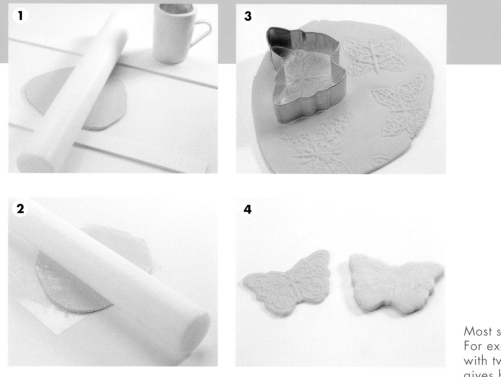

1

2

3

4

COOKIE CUTTERS WITH COORDINATING TEXTURE MATS

Some texture mats are designed to use with a cutter included with the mat. These sets make it easy to achieve a decorated cookie with nice detail. The covered cookies look great on their own, or color can be added using the instructions in the next section.

1 Brush a thin layer of piping gel on a baked and cooled cookie. A few cookies may be brushed at a time with the piping gel, but take note that the gel dries fairly quickly. Knead and soften rolled fondant. Lightly dust the work surface with powdered sugar to create a nonstick surface. Place the rolled fondant on the dusted surface between perfection strips. Roll over the strips, thinning the rolled fondant. Or use a rolling pin with rings. When rolling, lift and turn the rolled fondant a quarter turn. Do not turn the rolled fondant over. If the rolled fondant is sticking while lifting and turning, dust with additional powdered sugar

or knead powdered sugar into the rolled fondant to stiffen. Keep the top of the rolled fondant free of powdered sugar, or the covered cookie will have white spots or a white powdery finish.

2 Remove the perfection strips. Place a texture mat on the work surface. Many texture mats are double sided. One side will give a recessed impression, and the other a raised impression. Place the smooth, rolled side of the fondant facedown on the texture mat. Start on the end of the texture mat and roll over the rolled fondant with a generous amount of pressure.

3 Flip the texture mat with the rolled fondant over. Peel back the mat. Line up the cookie cutter with the textured piece of rolled fondant. Cut the rolled fondant.

4 Lift the cut shape and place on the cookie brushed with piping gel.

Most sets come with several mats. For example, the butterfly set comes with two texture mats. One mat gives butterfly impressions with whimsical, swirl designs. The other mat gives butterfly impressions with traditional butterfly patterns.

1

2

Food Color Markers

Some texture mats are better suited for this technique than others. The raised designs should be close together or the food color will likely seep onto the nonraised areas.

A food color marker may also be used for coloring raised areas. Allow several hours for the fondant-covered cookie to form a crust. Color the raised area holding a food color marker at a slight angle (approximately 15° angle) so the side of the marker, and not the tip, is applying the color. Holding the marker at a slight angle also makes it easier to keep the color off of the nonraised areas.

Another alternative is to cover the cookie with the design recessed in the rolled fondant. Allow several hours for the fondant-covered cookie to form a crust. Use a food color marker held at a 90° angle to color in the recessed area.

COLORING TEXTURED FONDANT

1 Follow instructions for covering a cookie with textured rolled fondant. Be sure to use the side of the texture mat so the details are raised when the mat is removed. Saturate a dry foam stamp pad (a small stamp pad with a handle is ideal) with liquid food color or airbrush food color. Use a paper towel to remove excess color. Test the color on a sheet of white paper.

2 Gently rub the saturated foam stamper over the raised area on the cookie.

FILLING IN RECESSED AREAS WITH RUN SUGAR

1 Follow the instructions for covering a cookie with textured rolled fondant. Be sure to use the side of the texture mat so the details are recessed when the mat is removed. Thin royal icing to achieve a run sugar consistency, following directions on page 62. Pour the run sugar into a parchment cone or a pastry bag fit with a small opening such as tip #2.

2 Pipe the thin icing into the recessed areas of the textured fondant.

USING TOOLS FOR TEXTURE

Cover the cookie with rolled fondant. Texture is added after the fondant is cut and placed on the cookie. Use various tools to texture the icing. The texture must be added immediately after covering the cookie or the fondant will crust and be difficult to texture. Do not cover all of the cookies with fondant at once, or the fondant will dry by the time the second or third cookie is ready to be textured. Cover the first cookie with fondant, then texture. Cover the second cookie with fondant, then texture, and so on.

A tip with a round opening held at a 45° angle works well for creating fish scales.

A tip with a round opening held at an 80° angle adds instant curls.

Holding a star tip and dragging the tip through the fondant creates grass, hair, or fur.

A ball tool adds round indentations for eyes or craters in the fondant.

A paring knife is used to emboss a V-shape in the round indentations for additional detail in the eye.

A paring knife adds line details. Note: Do not cut all the way through the rolled fondant.

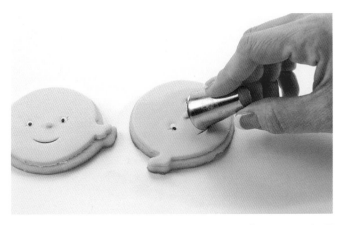

The wide end of a decorating tip works well to create half circles for happy or sad faces.

Embossers or detailed cutters can be pressed into the soft fondant for lovely details.

1

2

3

SHADING ROLLED FONDANT COOKIES

1 Cover the cookies with rolled fondant following the instructions in the previous section. Place the covered cookie on a sheet of parchment paper to make it easy to collect excess dust.

2 Brush the powder generously onto the area of the cookie that will be shaded. Shown is daffodil petal dust. Petal dust will provide a matte finish.

3 Add additional color if desired. The color can be brushed on top of the previous color to tone down the shade, or the color can be brushed on the edges. Shown is teal luster dust brushed over all. Luster dust gives a shimmery finish.

If your goal is to have a cookie with vibrant color, start with a light shade of rolled fondant in the desired tint, rather than starting with white rolled fondant. In the example, the butterfly is covered in a light green. Shading in yellow gives a yellow-green hue to the center of the butterfly.

STORING ROLLED FONDANT–COVERED COOKIES

Cookies covered with rolled fondant are best stored at room temperature and eaten within seven days. If the fondant-covered cookies will not be served within a day, store them in layers (if the designs are flat) or a single layer (if three-dimensional accents are added) in a loosely covered container. Do not refrigerate. If the container is tightly closed or if the container is placed in the refrigerator or freezer, condensation may form. Condensation may cause the rolled fondant to become sticky or spots may occur.

If the fondant-covered cookie is flat, then the cookies can be stacked or placed in cellophane bags. If the cookie has dainty rolled fondant accents such as flowers with shaped petals, the accents are delicate and may break if the cookies are stacked. Textured rolled fondant that has hardened slightly is resilient and holds up well even if the cookies are stacked. Before rolled fondant–covered cookies are stacked or placed in a bag, allow the rolled fondant to slightly harden (several hours).

You can ship rolled fondant–covered cookies if they don't have dainty details that may easily break when jostled.

Chocolate-Coated Cookies

Chocolate candy coating—often called confectionary coating, candy melts, almond bark, and summer coating—can be used as a delicious icing for cookies with a smooth, shiny finish. Candy coating is available in milk chocolate, dark chocolate, and white chocolate, as well as several colors.

Candy coating is different from chocolates with cocoa butter. Chocolate with cocoa butter must be tempered before coating the cookie or the chocolate will develop white streaks or will not set up properly. Tempering, which is not covered here, is a process of melting and cooling chocolate. Candy coating is much easier for the novice to use and comes ready to melt and use. The coating is thinner than other icings such as run sugar or buttercream. A squeeze bottle is used to apply the coating. Transfer sheets can be placed on the warm chocolate for a coating with a fun pattern in a contrasting color. Chocolate candy coating is very sensitive to heat and should be treated as you would a chocolate candy bar. Do not leave the chocolate-coated cookies in warm areas or the coating will melt.

MELTING CHOCOLATE AND CANDY COATINGS

Chocolates and coatings have a very low melting point. Watch carefully to prevent scorching. Keep water and steam away from chocolates and coatings. Note: These instructions are for melting candy coating. If making any of the projects included in this chapter with real chocolate, the chocolate must be tempered. Using a bowl with a squared edge allows the chocolate coating to be easily poured into squeeze bottles. Place chocolate wafers or coarsely chopped chocolate in a microwave-safe bowl. Microwave for 30 seconds. Stir. Continue microwaving only a few seconds at a time, stirring often, until chocolate is nearly melted. Remove from the microwave and stir until melted.

COLORING AND FLAVORING CHOCOLATE AND CANDY COATINGS

A wide variety of colored candy coating comes ready to use. If you'd like a color that is not available, color the candy with an oil-based food color. Food color gels, pastes, and liquids should not be used, as the chocolate may thicken when color is added. Powdered food colors may be used, but the powder should be dissolved in liquid vegetable shortening before adding to the chocolate. Powdered colors may give a speckled appearance to the coating. Oil-based and concentrated flavors can be added to the candy coating. Concentrated flavors tend to be about three times stronger than extracts. Add 12 to 15 drops per pound (0.54 kg). Avoid using extract and other water- or alcohol-based flavors used to flavor chocolates and coatings.

COATING COOKIES WITH CHOCOLATE USING A SQUEEZE BOTTLE

1 Pour the melted candy coating into a squeeze bottle. Trim tip of nozzle if necessary. Outline the baked and cooled cookie with the melted chocolate. Allow the outline to set for a few minutes.

2 After it is set, the outline will not be as shiny and is ready to be filled. Begin filling the outline, squeezing just enough candy coating for a thin layer. If too much candy coating is used, the candy will drip off the sides. The outline will often become warm and melt again when filling in the outline, so it does not provide a wall to prevent the candy coating from dripping off the sides.

3 Place cookie in the palm of your hand and tap to smooth.

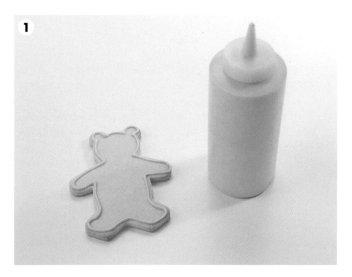

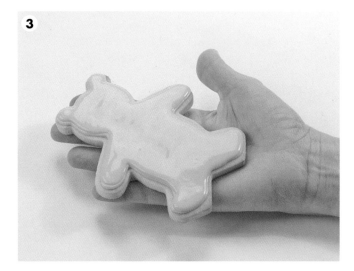

DIPPING COOKIES INTO CHOCOLATE COATING

1 Place the baked and cooled cookie into melted candy coating.

2 Push the cookie into the candy coating so that the cookie is completely immersed. After it is completely covered, bring the cookie out using a candy dipping tool. Tap the dipping tool on the bowl to smooth the top and allow excess candy coating to drip off the sides.

3 Scrape the bottom of the dipping tool along the edge of the bowl and place the cookie on a sheet of parchment paper. This creates a cookie that is completely hidden under a delicious coating of candy.

4 Allow the candy coating to dry for several minutes. If the candy coating has puddles, use scissors to trim excess coating.

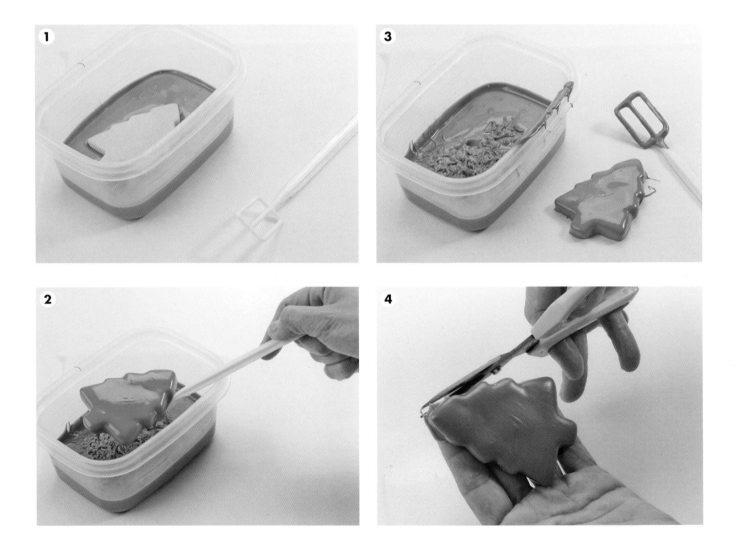

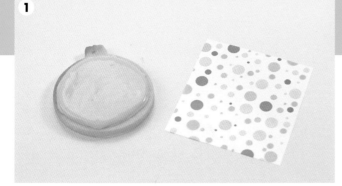

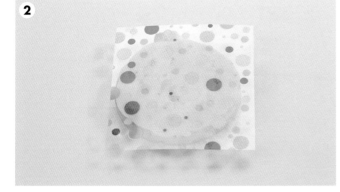

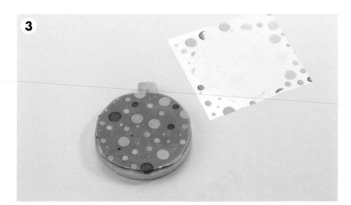

The color of the candy coating will change the design. The design will show up the best when the transfer sheet has a strong contrast with the candy coating. Shown are cookies covered with yellow candy coating, super white candy coating, and green candy coating.

Commercially available sandwich cookies or any cookie or cracker that is completely flat can be immersed in melted candy coating and decorated with transfer sheets for a quick and easy decorated cookie.

USING CHOCOLATE TRANSFER SHEETS

1 Cut a transfer sheet to fit the area that will be patterned. Follow instructions for Coating Cookies with Chocolate Using a Squeeze Bottle or Dipping Cookies into Chocolate Coating.

2 Immediately after the cookie is coated, place a transfer sheet on the warm coating, texture side down.

3 Allow the candy-coated cookies to set for several minutes. Remove the transfer sheet. For a shinier coating, place the baked cookies with the transfer sheet in the freezer for a few minutes instead of leaving them at room temperature to set.

Transfer Tips

Work quickly so the chocolate doesn't set before the transfer sheet is placed on the dipped cookie.

Working in a cool room, 72° F (22° C) or cooler, will provide the best results when using transfer sheets. If the room is too warm, the candy coating will appear dull after the transfer sheets are removed. If you can't avoid working in a warm room, place the cookies covered with candy coating and transfer sheets in the refrigerator for ten minutes before removing the sheets.

ADDING DETAILS

Pour melted candy coating into a parchment cone, a squeeze bottle with a fine tip attached, or a pastry bag fitted with a fine tip. A parchment cone without a tip is preferred. It is more difficult to unclog a squeeze bottle or pastry bag fitted with a small tip than a parchment cone without a tip. Touch the surface of the cookie and gently squeeze to release the candy coating. Because the coating is very fluid, it flows quickly from the bag or squeeze bottle and requires only minimal pressure.

Details can be piped onto the cookie with melted candy coating in a squeeze tube, called candy writers. The tubes are available in several colors and using them is much less messy than pouring candy coating into a bag. For fine details, a pastry bag or parchment cone with a smaller opening works better. These tubes of candy coating are ideal for kids to use when decorating cookies. Melt the candy in the tube by placing the tube in a heating pad or an electric skillet lined with towels (see tip opposite). You can also place the tube in the microwave, but take care to avoid burning the candy and the plastic tube. Melt the candy in the tube for a few seconds at a time, kneading in between intervals. Avoid trying to melt the tube under hot water, as the tip may become wet and if water gets into the tip, the chocolate will seize and become difficult to remove from the tube.

Sprinkles, premade sugar pieces (such as the snowflakes shown), or royal icing pieces can be immediately placed on the warm, coated cookie to "glue" the accents to the coating. If the candy coating has hardened, the edible decoration can be attached to the cookie with a bit of melted candy coating.

Unclogging

If the tips of the candy writers, squeeze bottles, or pastry bag fitted with a tip become clogged, unclog with a straight pin.

STORING CANDY-COATED COOKIES

Store cookies coated with chocolate or candy coating at room temperature and eat within seven days. If the iced cookies will not be served within a day, store them in layers in a loosely covered container. Do not refrigerate. If the container is tightly closed or if the container is placed in the refrigerator or freezer, condensation may form. Condensation may cause the chocolate or candy coating to become tacky.

Candy-coated cookies dry quickly and may be stacked or placed in individual bags within an hour or two after they are decorated.

Candy-coated cookies ship well in cooler temperatures. The firm coating makes them more resistant to breakage than other icings. However, like a candy bar, the candy coating will melt in warm temperatures. Keep in mind that it is warmer inside delivery trucks and shipping warehouses than outside temperatures.

Stay Warm

Keep the bowls of melted chocolate, filled squeeze bottles, parchment cones, and candy writers warm by placing them in an electric skillet lined with several dry towels; set the skillet on the lowest setting. The skillet should be warm to touch, but not too hot or the chocolate will cook and burn instead of melt. Bottles and candy writers can also be placed in a heating pad set to low to keep the chocolate warm.

Egg Wash Glaze

This simple icing is achieved by mixing egg whites and powdered sugar. Pasteurized egg whites can be used to eliminate the risk of salmonella. Egg wash glaze is a thin glaze used primarily for molded cookies. It provides a subtle sheen and a smooth coating to cookies without compromising the details. The glaze is brushed on the baked and cooled cookie. Allow at least an hour for the glaze to dry before painting on details. Very little sweetness is produced using this icing. If additional sweetness is desired, coat the back of the cookie with buttercream, page 82, or candy coating, page 114.

Recipe

- *1 egg white*
- *½ cup (65 g) powdered sugar*

Whisk the egg white until light and fluffy. Stir in powdered sugar. Whisk until the sugar is dissolved. Brush glaze onto the baked and cooled cookie.

PAINTING THE COOKIE

1 Glaze the cookie with the egg wash glaze. Allow at least an hour for the glaze to dry. When the egg wash glaze is completely dry, the cookie is ready to be painted. Fill each cavity of a paint tray half full of water. Squirt small amounts of food color gel onto the top of a paint tray. Blend some of the food color gel with the water in the cavities until the desired shade is achieved. Test the color on a white sheet of paper.

2

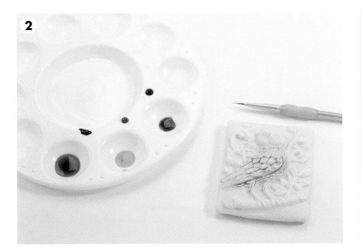

Food color markers with a fine tip can be used with or instead of the thinned food color.

3

2 Use a fine brush with rounded bristles and paint the details.

3 Blend the concentrated food color on the top of the paint tray with a small amount of water to create a thick, dark paint for shading. Test the color on a white sheet of paper. Use the shading color to add contrast and shading to the cookie.

STORING EGG WASH–GLAZED COOKIES

Cookies glazed with the egg wash glaze can be stored at room temperature and are best eaten within two or three days. Place the cookies in layers in a loosely covered container.

The egg wash–glazed and painted cookies can be arranged on a serving plate or placed in cellophane bags after the painting has completely dried (allow at least 6 hours). If the food color was not thinned with water, the painted cookie may remain sticky and leave residue in the cellophane bags.

Gallery

If you would like materials lists and complete directions for making any of these cookies, please visit http://www.creativepub.com/pages/cookiedecorating or www.cookiedecorating.com

Baby Girl Cookies: Run Sugar, page 64; and Detailed Piping with Royal Icing, page 74

Blue Bootie Cookies: Chocolate-Coated Cookies, page 114

Graduation Cookies: Run Sugar, page 64; Marbled Run Sugar, page 71; and Detailed Piping with Royal Icing, page 74

Jungle Animal Cookies: Run Sugar, page 64; and Detailed Piping with Royal Icing, page 74

Jungle Animal Faces Cookies: Chocolate-Coated Cookies, page 114

Little Insect Cookies: Chocolate-Coated Cookies, page 114

Peace and Love Cookies: Cookie Cutter Shapes, page 23; Run Sugar, page 64; Marbled Run Sugar, page 71; and Detailed Piping with Royal Icing, page 74

Kitties and Mice Cookies: Run Sugar, page 64; and Detailed Piping with Royal Icing, page 74

Rock and Roll Cookies: Cookie Cutter Shapes, page 23; Run Sugar, page 64; Marbled Run Sugar, page 71; Detailed Piping with Royal Icing, page 74; and Shimmery, Sparkly Cookies, page 130

Pirate Cookies: Cookie Cutter Shapes, page 23; Run Sugar, page 64; Marbled Run Sugar, page 71; and Detailed Piping with Royal Icing, page 74

Sports Ball Cookies: Rolled Fondant, page 100

Painted Ladybugs: Painted Cookies, page 78

Painted Nature Cookies: Egg Wash Glaze, page 120; and Shimmery, Sparkly Cookies, page 130

Paris Themed Cookies: Run Sugar, page 64; and Detailed Piping with Royal Icing, page 74

Marbled Valentine Cookies: Run Sugar, page 64; Marbled Run Sugar, page 71; and Detailed Piping with Royal Icing, page 74

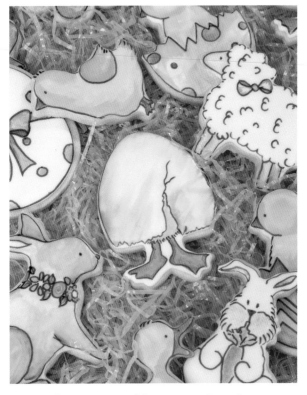

Painted Easter Cookies: Painted Cookies, page 78

Faces of Halloween Cookies: Rolled Fondant, page 100; Detailed Piping with Royal Icing, page 74; and Shimmery, Sparkly cookies, page 130

Owl Cookies: Cookie Cutter Shapes, page 23; Run Sugar, page 64; and Detailed Piping with Royal Icing, page 74

Wintertime Cookies: Run Sugar, page 64; and Detailed Piping with Royal Icing, page 74

Christmas Light Cookies: Run Sugar, page 64

Gingerbread Boys and Girls: Chocolate-Coated Cookies, page 114

Santa and Reindeer: Run Sugar, page 64; Marbled Run Sugar, page 71; and Detailed Piping with Royal Icing, page 74

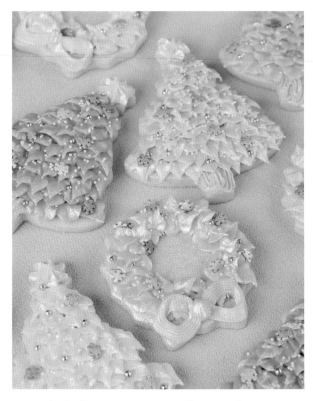

Pastel Christmas Trees and Wreaths: Buttercream Icing, page 82; and Shimmery, Sparkly Cookies, page 130

Painted Christmas Cookies: Egg Wash Glaze, page 120

MISCELLANEOUS TECHNIQUES

Now that you have learned the basic cookie decorating skills, take some time to try out the techniques in this section to discover additional decorating methods. Several of the techniques covered in this chapter require a base icing, such as rolled fondant or run sugar. After the cookie is iced, additional details are added using various techniques such as flocking, brush embroidery, rolled fondant accents, or stencils.

Shimmery, Sparkly Cookies

There are a variety of products commercially available to add shimmer and sparkle to cookies. Some products are approved by the United States Food and Drug Administration (FDA), others are nontoxic but do not yet have FDA approval for human consumption. Some of the products not approved in the United States, such as dusting powders, are approved in other countries as a food product. Dusting powers are fine powders that can be brushed on dry. Luster dusts are available in classic metallics, such as gold, silver, and copper, as well as several colors with a shimmer. Pearl dusts have a white pearl shimmer. Platinum dusts are dusts that are FDA approved with a white shimmer. Petal dusts provide a matte finish. Dusting powders work on any icing that completely sets. Brushing the dust on while dry will give an all-over shimmer. To create a confined metallic area, make a paint with the dusting powder. When brushing dusting powders onto cookies, the grain is not visible. Another product that does not show grains is metallic food sprays. Using metallic food spray is the best way to achieve an all-over shimmer to buttercream-iced cookies. Edible glitter is small, flavorless flakes that sparkle under light. Disco dust, also called mystical dust or fairy dust, is the product that provides the most sparkle but is recommended for decorative use only. Sanding sugar has a coarse grain and is fun to use for sparkle and added crunch. Coarse sugar is used for even more sparkle and crunch, but can look a bit heavy on small cookies. Instructions are also included in this chapter to custom color sanding sugars and sprinkles. When sprinkling sugars or brushing dusts on cookies, place the cookie on parchment paper to gather excess sugar and dust. Form the parchment in a V-shape to funnel the sugar and dust back into the container.

COOKIES BRUSHED WITH DUSTING POWDERS

1 Decorate the cookies as desired. Allow the icing to completely dry. Place the decorated cookie on a sheet of parchment to catch excess dust.

2

COOKIES PAINTED WITH DUSTING POWDERS

1 Mix the dry dusting powder in a paint tray with a small amount of grain spirits. Add just enough spirits to turn the powder into a paint. Note: Lemon oil, not to be confused with lemon juice, may be used in place of the grain spirits. However, the metallic will be slightly less intense with lemon oil.

2 Paint the details with the metallic paint.

3

1

2 Dip a large, dry brush with soft, round bristles into the dusting powder. Tap the brush against the dusting powder jar to release excess powder. Brush the cookie with the dusting powder. Note: Cookies covered in rolled fondant can be dusted with dusting powders at any time. It is not necessary to wait for the rolled fondant to harden.

3 Continue brushing the cookie with the dust until the cookie is completely covered. Form a cone with the parchment paper and pour the excess dust back into the container.

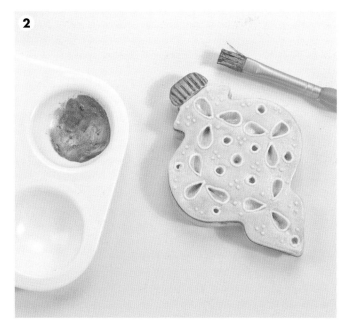

2

Avoid Brush Strokes

If the cookie is iced with buttercream, the brush may give bristle indentations. To avoid this, freeze the decorated cookies for a few minutes, and bring out one cookie at a time and dust with the powder.

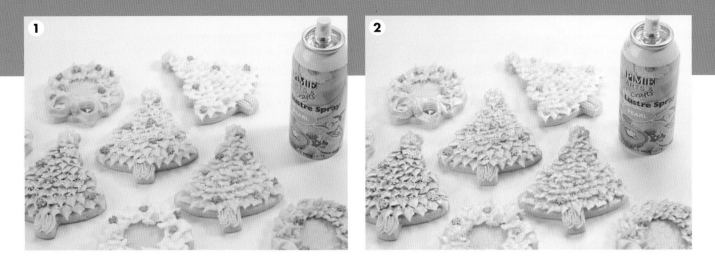

COOKIES SPRAYED WITH METALLIC SPRAYS

1 Arrange decorated cookies close together on a sheet of parchment paper.

2 Hold the can of metallic food color about 12" (30.5 cm) from the cookies. Spray the cookies while slowly and steadily moving your hand back and forth a few times.

COOKIES WITH SANDING SUGAR

(*See also* Flocking, page 138.)

1 Ice the cookie with the desired icing. Place the iced cookie on a sheet of parchment to catch excess sugar.

2 While the icing is still wet, sprinkle with sanding sugar.

3 Lift the cookie and turn over to remove excess sugar.

Sanding

If the icing has crusted or if rolled fondant is used, brush a thin layer of piping gel onto the crusted icing or rolled fondant. Sprinkle the sanding sugar on the piping gel.

CUSTOM SUGAR COLORS

1 Pour white sanding sugar in a large ziplock bag. Regular granulated sugar may be used, but the sparkle will be very subtle. Pour a small amount of powdered food color or dusting powder into the ziplock bag. The amount of color used will depend on the shade desired. Start with a small amount of color and add more powdered color until achieving the desired shade.

2 Shake the bag to spread the color.

White sprinkles, nonpareils, jimmies, and sugars all color well with powdered food colors. These white snowflakes were coated in peacock blue dusting powder.

1

Shiny, pearlized, or candy-coated pieces will cover the sprinkles with a very thin coating of color, giving a muted shade. The pearlized sugar pearls were coated with super red luster dust.

2

Custom Color with Gel

Gel food color can be used to custom color sugars. Squeeze a small amount of gel food color onto the white sanding sugar. Squeeze and shake the bag to spread the color. The water in the food color may cause the colored sanding sugar to clump as it dries and evaporates. Simply squeeze the bag to remove any clumps before applying the sanding sugar.

EDIBLE GLITTER

1 Ice the cookie with the desired icing. In this example, the tree was iced in run sugar. The green and brown run sugar has completely set.

2 Pipe icing onto the area that is to be coated with glitter.

3 While the icing is still wet, sprinkle the icing with edible glitter.

4 Lift the cookie and turn over to remove excess glitter.

Piping Gel

If the icing has crusted or if rolled fondant is used, brush a thin layer of piping gel onto the crusted icing. Add the edible glitter to the piping gel.

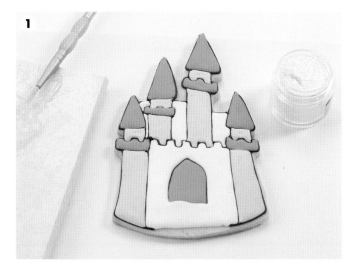

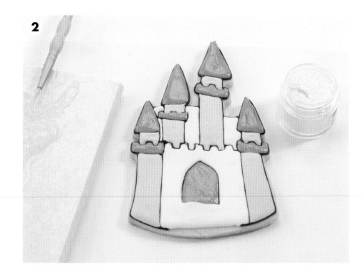

DISCO DUST

1 Allow the icing on the cookie to completely set. Place the cookie on a sheet of parchment to collect excess dust. Mix piping gel with a small amount of water to create a thin glaze.

2 Brush the area to be glittered with piping gel.

Disco Over Wet

Disco dust may be sprinkled onto wet icing; however, the super fine particles of disco dust may absorb into the icing. If the dust absorbs into the icing, add more dust and note that the texture of the particles will be noticeable when bitten.

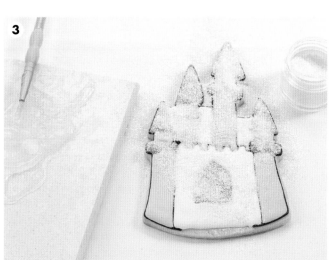

3 Sprinkle the piping gel with disco dust.

4 Lift the cookie and turn over to remove excess dust.

Eyelet Decorating

Add a dainty lace effect to cookies using small cutters and embossers. Cover the eyelet cookies with two layers of rolled fondant in contrasting colors. For the best tasting decorated cookie, the baked cookie should be about twice as thick as the layered rolled fondant. Pipe royal icing around the cutouts using a tip with a small opening for the final touch. When mixing the royal icing for piping, be sure to sift the powdered ingredients through a mesh sifter with very fine screen to ensure the tip does not get clogged when piping.

1 Knead and soften two colors of rolled fondant. Lightly dust the work surface with powdered sugar. Place one color of rolled fondant on the dusted surface between two perfection strips, 2 mm thick. Roll over the strips, thinning the rolled fondant. When rolling, lift and turn the rolled fondant a quarter turn to prevent the pieces from sticking. Do not turn the rolled fondant over. If the fondant is sticking while lifting and turning, dust with additional powdered sugar or knead powdered sugar into the rolled fondant to stiffen. Keep the top of the rolled fondant free of powdered sugar, or the covered cookie will have white spots or a white powdery finish. Repeat the rolling process with the second color of rolled fondant.

2 Place one color of rolled fondant on top of the other. Roll over the layered fondant one roll, causing the pieces to adhere to one another. Test to see if the rolled fondant layers are sticking together. If not, brush a very small amount of water on top of the bottom layer. Brush a thin layer of piping gel on the baked and cooled cookie. Cut the rolled fondant with the same cutter that was used for the cookie. Lift the shape and place on the cookie brushed with piping gel.

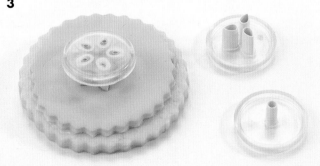

3 Press an eyelet cutter into the rolled fondant–covered cookie. The cutter should cut completely through the first layer, but not the second layer. Do not press too firmly, or the cookie may break.

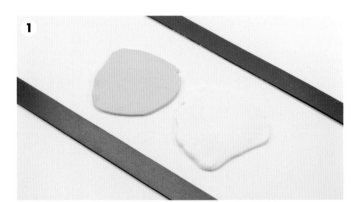

4

6

5

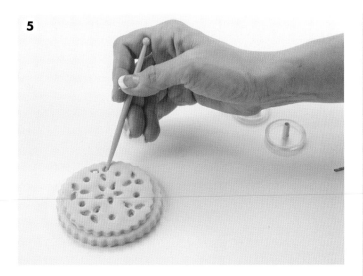

4 Lift the eyelet cutter and remove cut pieces of the top rolled fondant layer, using a toothpick or a needle tool. If the cookie is showing through the cut shape, the cutter was pressed into the second layer of fondant.

5 Press a ball tool into the cut designs to soften the cutouts and blend the top layer with the bottom.

6 Pipe around the cutouts and add details using royal icing and tip #1.

Modeling tools may also be used to create an eyelet pattern. Hold the cone tool at a 45° angle and press into the layered fondant. A ball tool or the end of a brush can be used to emboss small round eyelet openings. Hold the ball tool at a 90° angle and press into the layered fondant.

Flocking

Flocking is a technique of decorating cookies using small specks of fine edible sprinkles to create a contrasting velvety outline or pattern. Sanding sugar is most commonly used for flocking, but other edible particles may be used. Regular table sugar (granulated sugar) can be used, though it will not produce as much sparkle.

To create a contrasting textured pattern, the base icing must form a crust. After the base icing has crusted, details are piped and the edible sprinkles are added. If the base icing has not crusted, the edible sprinkles stick to the entire iced cookie. The outlining icing and the flocking sugar should be very close in color. For example, white icing may show through if cookies are outlined in white royal icing and are flocked with red sanding sugar. The cookie should be outlined in red royal icing and flocked with red sanding sugar. Sanding sugar can be placed in a squeeze bottle with a large hole cut to easily disperse the sugar.

FLOCKED RUN SUGAR OUTLINE

1 Ice the cookie with run sugar. Allow the icing to harden several hours or overnight. Place the cookie on a sheet of parchment paper or a cookie sheet with sides. Fit a pastry bag with a #2 tip. Fill the pastry bag with medium-consistency royal icing. Hold the pastry bag at a 45° angle. Touch the iced cookie and squeeze to attach the icing. While still squeezing, lift the pastry bag and begin outlining the cookie. Continue outlining while applying steady pressure. Touch the surface and stop squeezing to attach the end of the outline.

Little at a Time

If the cookie will have a lot of outlining, outline a small amount at a time. Otherwise, part of the outline may set before the sugar is added.

1

2

2 Sprinkle sanding sugar onto the wet outline. Turn the cookie over to allow the excess sugar to fall from the cookie onto the parchment sheet. The sugar will only adhere to the wet outline.

3 Allow several hours or overnight for the outline to harden. Then remove any excess sugar using a soft brush.

3

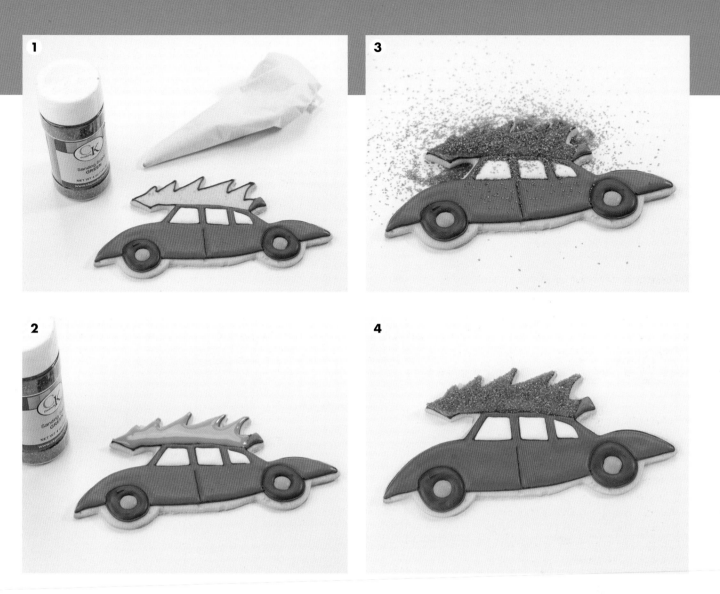

FLOCKED RUN SUGAR AREAS

1 Decorate the part of the cookie that will not be flocked using run sugar icing. Allow several hours for the run sugar to harden. Place the cookie on a sheet of parchment paper or a cookie sheet with sides.

2 Pipe the areas that will be flocked with run sugar.

3 Immediately sprinkle the wet icing with sanding sugar.

4 Turn the cookie over, allowing excess sugar to fall from the cookie and onto the parchment sheet or cookie sheet. The sugar will only adhere to the wet areas. Allow several hours or overnight for the flocked icing area to harden. Then remove any excess sugar using a soft brush.

If you are using more than one color of flocking sugar, such as in the bumblebee cookie, sprinkle the sugar on wet icing rather than using the piping gel method. Sprinkle the sugar on the first color of icing and allow several hours for the icing to dry. When the first flocked color is completely set, the second color can be piped and flocked.

Rolled fondant may be used in place of run sugar for the base icing on the cookie. Royal icing is used to pipe the outline.

Buttercream may also be used in place of run sugar. Be sure the buttercream crusts completely before flocking an outline or select area. For a flocked outline, follow the same instructions as above, only substitute buttercream for the royal icing.

Candy coating may also be used in place of run sugar for either flocking method. For a flocked outline, coat the cookie with candy coating and allow it to set for several minutes. Pour melted candy coating in a parchment cone, pastry bag with tip #2 attached, or a squeeze bottle. Candy coating will flow much quicker than royal icing or buttercream, so use a gentle touch when squeezing the pastry bag. The outline will set quicker than buttercream or royal icing.

Sanding sugars are not the only type of sprinkles that can be used for flocking. The Santa hat has jimmies on one hat and nonpareils on the other.

Flocking Tips

- If the icing has hardened, or if rolled fondant is used, brush the area of the cookie to be flocked with piping gel. Sprinkle sanding sugar onto the piping gel. Turn the cookie over to allow the excess sugar to fall onto the parchment sheet or cookie sheet. The sugar will only adhere to the piping gel areas.

- Flocking sugars with super-fine particles, such as disco dust, may absorb into the wet icing. If this happens, add more dust and note that the texture of the particles will be noticeable when bitten.

- Hold the cookie over parchment paper or a cookie sheet with sides to contain and easily gather excess sugar.

- Put sanding sugar in a squeeze bottle for better control of the sugar and less mess.

Brush Embroidery

Brush embroidery creates a cookie with an elegant lace design. It is achieved by piping stiff, but fluffy, royal icing and then pulling the icing with a flat brush to create texture. Brushstrokes should be visible. The background color should show through toward the center of the petal. If brushstrokes are not visible, the royal icing may be too thin. Add more powdered sugar and whip to stiffen the royal icing. Classic brush embroidery is achieved using white royal icing. Brush embroidery can be piped onto rolled fondant–covered cookies or run sugar–glazed cookies. Use tip #3 for adding brush embroidery to 2" to 4" (5.1 to 10.2 cm) flowers . Use tip #1 or #2 for smaller flowers, and tips with larger openings, such as tip #4 or #5 for flowers larger than 5" (12.7 cm).

BRUSH EMBROIDERY ON FLOWER-SHAPED COOKIES

1

2

3

1 Cover the baked and cooled cookie with rolled fondant or run sugar. Fit a pastry bag with tip #3, and fill the bag with stiff royal icing. Outline one petal with the royal icing.

2 Immediately after piping, gently touch the top of the outline with a damp, flat brush. Hold the brush at a 45° angle. With long strokes, drag the royal icing toward the center of the petal. The brushed icing should be thick where the outline starts and thin toward the center.

3 Repeat, outlining and brushing one petal at a time. Brush every other petal to allow adjoining petals time to harden. The royal icing may harden if too many petals are outlined at once. Add additional piped details. The center of the flower looks nice with one dot or with a cluster of several small piped dots.

The brush embroidery outline is typically piped with white royal icing. Outlining the flower petals with colored royal icing gives cookies a modern, stylized design.

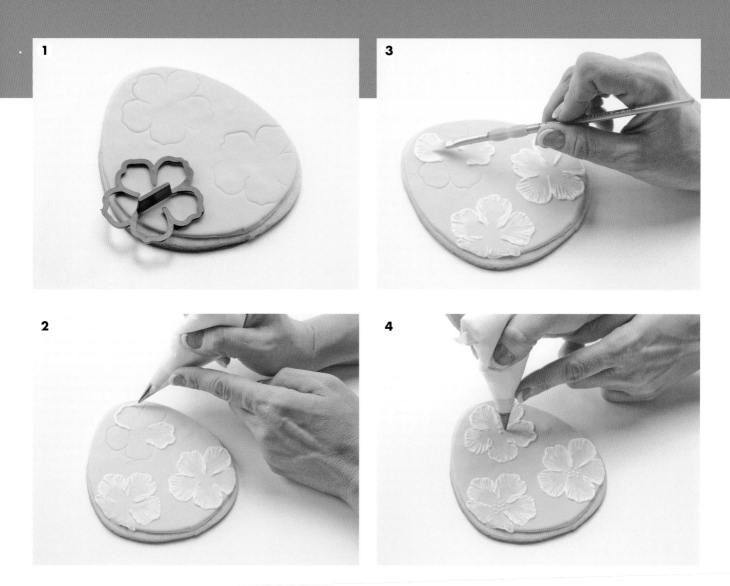

BRUSH EMBROIDERY WITH EMBOSSED FLOWERS

1 Cover the baked and cooled cookie with rolled fondant. Then immediately emboss the rolled fondant with a flower cutter. The rolled fondant must be soft when embossing or the rolled fondant will crack. For best results, cover one cookie at a time with rolled fondant or cover a few and keep them tightly covered with plastic wrap until ready to emboss.

2 Fit a pastry bag with tip #3, and fill the bag with stiff royal icing. Outline one petal of the embossed flower with the royal icing.

Mind the Brush

Be sure to keep the brush clean and damp when brushing the royal icing. Keep a bowl of water to rinse the brush. After rinsing, wipe off excess water with a damp towel.

3 Immediately after piping, gently touch the top of the outline with a damp, flat brush. Hold the brush at a 45° angle. With long strokes, drag the royal icing toward the center of the petal. The brushed icing should be thick where the outline starts and thin toward the center.

4 Repeat, outlining and brushing one petal at a time. The royal icing may harden if too many petals are outlined at once. Add additional piped details. The center of the flower looks nice with one dot or with a cluster of several small piped dots.

If run sugar is desired instead of rolled fondant, cover the cookie with run sugar icing and pipe royal icing freehand, or add the design using the perfect lettering or artwork method on page 148.

Stencils

A stencil adds color and dimension quickly. It is important the cookie's surface is as smooth and flat as possible. Rolled fondant–covered or run sugar–iced cookies produce the best results when using stencils, but other icings may be used. The run sugar–iced cookie must harden completely before using stencils. While buttercream may also be used, the details will not be as sharp and crisp. Allow the buttercream several hours to crust. Use buttercream icing instead of royal icing to add the details with the stencil.

ADDING A PATTERN WITH ICING

1 Mix royal icing according to directions on page 60. If necessary, thin the royal icing with water so the royal icing has a soft peak. Place stencil on the iced cookie.

2 Put a small scoop of royal icing on one end of the stencil.

3 Spread the royal icing along the stencil using a small scraper or a spatula with a thin blade.

4 Peel back the stencil.

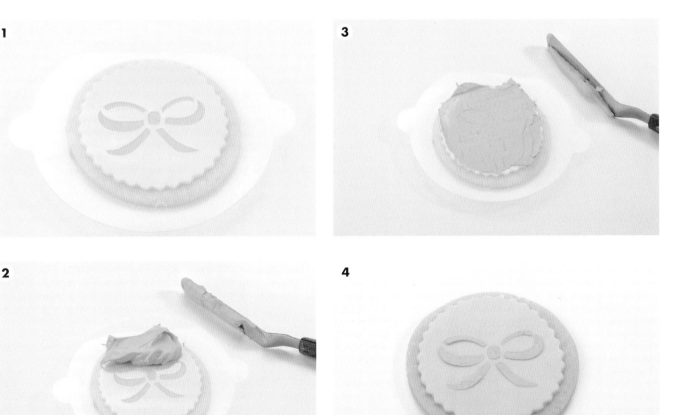

ADDING A PATTERN WITH FOOD COLOR

It's easy to add a design to an iced cookie with stencils and food color. A stencil brush is used to apply the color. It is important that the rolled fondant has hardened, or the brush will imprint grooves into the fondant. For best results, stencil the cookie a day after covering with the rolled fondant. A cookie iced with run sugar also provides a nice, smooth surface for stenciling. Be sure the run sugar is as smooth and even as possible.

1 Cover the cookie with white rolled fondant or white run sugar. Allow the rolled fondant or run sugar to set for several hours or overnight. Pour food color in a cavity of a paint tray. Add a touch of water to thin the food color slightly.

2 Dip the stencil brush into the food color. Wipe off excess color onto a paper towel or a piece of paper. This will also show the color that will be applied. If the color is too concentrated, add white food color to soften it. Place the stencil on top of the iced cookie. Keep the stencil steady with your nondominant hand. Dab the brush against the stencil with your other hand. Thoroughly wash the brush before applying additional colors.

3 Lift the stencil straight up.

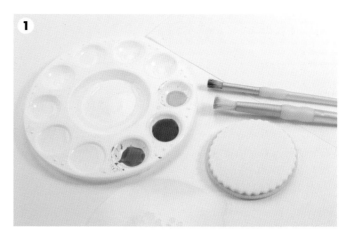

Steady the Stencil

If the stencil is moving while adding color, rub a small amount of solid vegetable shortening on the back of the stencil. Use very little shortening, as the grease may spot the rolled fondant or run sugar.

Edible Frosting Sheets

Edible frosting sheets—pictures printed on edible paper with food color—will add a fun, vibrant pattern to cookies. The sheets do not have flavor or texture and will absorb into wet icings, such as buttercream or run sugar. These sheets are easy to apply and are one of the simplest techniques to quickly decorate a cookie. Edible sheets come in side designs, full sheet designs, and ribbons. Full sheet designs allow the most flexibility. They are sized approximately 8" x 10" (20.3 x 25.4 cm) and will cover several 2" to 3" (5.1 to 7.6 cm) cookies. Side designs work well for small cookies or for adding sections of patterns on large cookies. Side designs are typically in 2½" x 10" (6.4 x 25.4 cm) strips. Ribbons can be added for a quick stripe of color.

You can buy printers with edible ink cartridges to print edible pictures from home, though such printers may be a costly investment. Check with your local cake and candy supply stores to see if they print customer's pictures. If printing photos taken by a professional photographer or if copyright information is written on the back, obtain the photographer's permission to print the image.

The edible frosting sheets absorb into the icing with moisture. If the cookie is iced in a color, the colored icing may change the tint of the edible print. For example, if a cookie is iced in pink icing, all white areas may turn pink. All yellow areas may turn orange. White icing will not affect the color of the edible print.

It is important to store edible frosting sheets properly. Keep the frosting sheets tightly sealed in a plastic bag at room temperature. If the edible frosting sheets are difficult to remove from the paper backing, place in the freezer for 2 minutes.

INSTRUCTIONS FOR BUTTERCREAM OR RUN SUGAR-ICED COOKIES

1

2

3

1 Place the same cutter that was used for baking the cookie on top of the edible frosting sheet. With an edible marker, trace around the cookie cutter. A cookie baked using a cutter with few angles is easier to cover with an edible frosting sheet than a cookie with many angles.

2 Cut the frosting sheet following the edible marker outline. With the design facing up, slide the edible frosting sheet over the edge of a countertop to release the design. Pipe icing onto the cookie.

3 Remove the image from paper backing and place the edible frosting sheet on the iced cookie. Gently smooth by pressing the frosting sheet with your palm, taking care not to shift the image.

Won't Stick

If the buttercream or run sugar has crusted, the edible sheet may not adhere to the cookie. Brush a thin layer of piping gel onto the crusted or hardened icing to allow the sheet to adhere.

Colored icings show through the white areas and will likely tints the colored areas of the frosting sheet. This pumpkin cookie is iced in orange buttercream. The edible frosting sheet is white with black swirls.

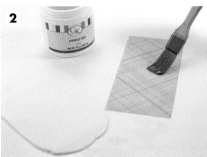

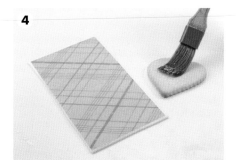

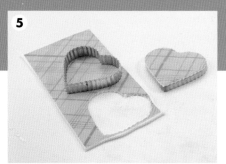

INSTRUCTIONS FOR ROLLED FONDANT–COVERED COOKIES

1 Roll enough rolled fondant to fit the frosting sheet, rolling to 2 mm thickness. Remove frosting sheet from the paper backing.

2 Turn over the frosting sheet. Brush the back of the frosting sheet with a thin layer of piping gel.

3 Place the frosting sheet on the rolled fondant. Gently roll over the fondant with minimal pressure to completely attach. To eliminate wasting the non-patterned rolled fondant, use a pizza cutter to remove fondant that extended past the frosting sheet and wrap tightly.

4 Brush the baked and cooled cookie with piping gel.

5 Use the same cutter used for baking the cookie to cut patterned fondant. Gently lift the cut shapes and place on piping gel–coated cookies. Take care when lifting the pieces to avoid wrinkling the frosting sheet.

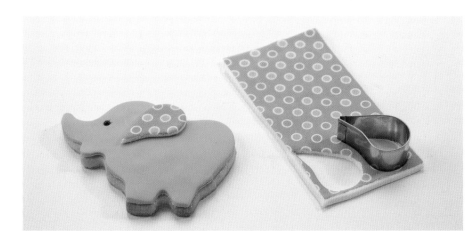

Small pieces of patterned fondant can be cut to create a cookie with patterned sections. Cut small sections of the frosting sheets and adhere to rolled fondant. Cut shapes and attach to the cookie with piping gel.

Perfect Lettering or Artwork

When several cookies will have the same design, it's best to use a pattern. Cookies with uniform artwork look more professional. You can also use a pattern to achieve perfect lettering on a cookie.

We'll cover two methods to achieving perfect designs. The pencil method, best used on light colored icings, uses a nontoxic pencil to put a very faint print onto a cookie with a hardened icing. Note that while nontoxic supplies are used, this method is not yet food approved. For a technique that is considered food safe, use the pinprick method. The pinprick method works well on buttercream-iced cookies, chocolate-covered cookies, just-covered rolled fondant cookies, or cookies that have hardened run sugar icing. In these two methods, after the artwork or lettering has been transferred, the faint pencil marking or tiny holes are used as a guide for piping royal icing. In either the pencil or pinprick method, the design can be outlined with run sugar for a strong, visible outline (shown on the princess cookie), or it can be piped in run sugar without an outline (shown on the monkey cookies). Refer to Run Sugar, page 64, for more on using this icing. If using the pencil method, food color markers can be used to color the design.

PLAN THE DESIGN

1 Outline the cookie cutter using a pencil and draw the design details inside the outline. A design can be as simple as a few swirls and dots, or it can be elaborate with several details. Draw the design by hand or trace clip art printed from a computer, a picture from a coloring book, scrapbook paper, stickers, and so on. To achieve perfect lettering, use word processing software to print the size and font style desired. If the lettering or artwork is not hand drawn using a pencil, you'll need to trace the design with a nontoxic pencil so it can be transferred. If the design includes text, the back of the paper will need to be outlined so that mirrored letters are traced and the letters will be transferred correctly.

2 Cut the paper following the cookie cutter outline. Follow the instructions for the pencil or pinprick method.

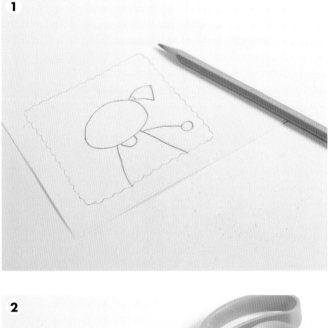

PENCIL METHOD

1 Bake and cool the cookies. Ice the cookies with desired icing. Allow the run sugar icing to harden or the rolled fondant to crust overnight. Follow steps 1 and 2 opposite. Turn the paper over with the pencil design on top of the icing.

2 Scribble over the design, taking care that the paper does not slip.

3 Remove the paper; the design will be very faint.

4 Trace over the letters or artwork by piping run sugar using a tip with a small round opening. Tip #1 works well for 2" to 4" (5.1 to 10.2 cm) cookies Tip #1.5 or #2 are good for larger cookies. Tip #0 is a dainty size for small cookies. See page 74 for detailed piping tips and instructions.

(continued)

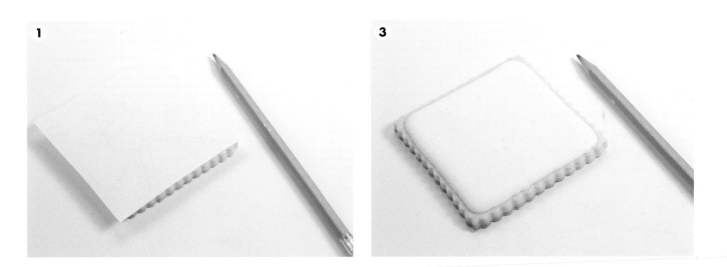

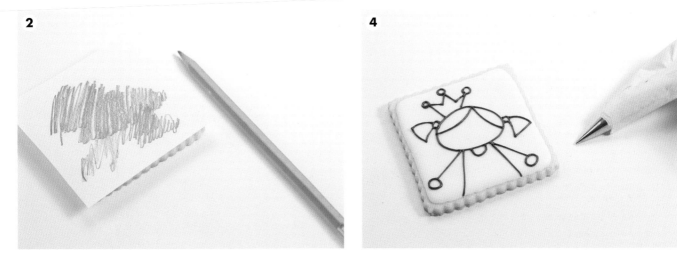

5

5. Fill in the outline with run sugar in the desired colors.

6. If additional details are needed, such as the little girl's face, allow the colored run sugar to set. Repeat the tracing steps.

6

A food color marker can be used instead of run sugar. Simply trace over the letters or artwork.

PINPRICK METHOD

1 This method can be used on rolled fondant that is soft, buttercream icing that has crusted, run sugar that has hardened, or chocolate-coated cookies that are set. If rolled fondant is used, the design should be pricked as soon as the cookie has been covered with the fondant and it is still soft. Follow steps 1 and 2 on page 148. Place the paper on the cookie, right side up. Use a pin to prick the design into the icing, taking care that the paper does not slip.

2 Remove the paper to reveal the pinhole pattern on the cookie.

3 Pipe run sugar icing following the pinprick pattern.

4 If additional details are needed, such as the features on the monkey's face, allow the colored run sugar to set. Repeat the tracing steps.

A Kopykake machine is a useful tool for production or commercial decorating when dozens of cookies will be duplicated. The artwork is put into the Kopykake cabinet, and the cookie is decorated following the artwork projected onto the cookie.

Accenting Cookies with Rolled Fondant

Add accents and fine details with rolled fondant. These accents can be applied on nearly any icing, including buttercream, chocolate, or rolled fondant–covered cookies. All of the cookies with accents in this book were made using rolled fondant. See page 100 for the recipe and more information about rolled fondant. Or, use gum paste to make accents with rolled fondant.

Although gum paste is not harmful to eat, note that the pieces will dry very hard. Cookies should not be covered with gum paste. I rarely use gum paste when decorating cookies—unless the cookies are for a project that will not be eaten, such as Christmas ornaments. When the cookies are for art and not consumption, gum paste has several advantages. It dries harder and is less fragile than rolled fondant. Gum paste can also be rolled thinner than rolled fondant, producing flowers with very fine petals. If creating pieces for cookies that will be consumed and a very delicate accent is desired, consider using a 50/50 paste of rolled fondant and gum paste. This is the best of both worlds, producing accent pieces with finer details than rolled fondant but not drying as hard as gum paste. This chapter includes two recipes for gum paste as well as instructions making a 50/50 paste. Gum paste is also available in a mix—simply add water. Whether using rolled fondant, gum paste, or 50/50 paste, it is crucial to keep the paste covered at all times to prevent crusting. Gum paste and 50/50 paste can be colored the same as rolled fondant, see page 51. Remember, if any of the pastes are overworked, they will become stiff and toughen. A touch of shortening or egg whites can be added to soften the paste. To attach the accents to the cookie, use Tylose glue or piping gel.

RECIPES

Nicholas Lodge's Gum Paste Recipe

- 4⅜ ounces (125 g) fresh egg whites
- 1 pound 9 ounces (700 g) powdered sugar
- additional 9 ounces (250 g) powdered sugar
- 1¼ ounce (35 g) Tylose powder
- ¾ ounce (20 g) solid vegetable shortening

Place the egg whites in a mixer bowl fitted with the flat paddle. Turn the mixer on high speed for 10 seconds to break up the egg whites. Turn the mixer to the lowest speed; slowly add the 700 grams of powdered sugar. This will make a soft-consistency royal icing. Turn up the speed to setting 3 or 4 for about 2 minutes. Make sure the mixture is at the soft-peak stage. It should look shiny, like meringue, and the peaks should fall over. If coloring the whole batch, add the paste or gel food color at this stage, making it a shade darker than the desired color. Turn the mixer to the slow setting and sprinkle the Tylose in over a 5-second time period. Turn the speed up to the high setting for a few seconds. This will thicken the mixture. Scrape the mixture out of the bowl onto a work surface that has been sprinkled with some of the 250 g of powdered sugar. Rub shortening on your hands and knead the paste, adding enough of the reserved powdered sugar to form a soft but not sticky dough. Check the consistency by pinching the dough with your fingers. Your fingers should come away clean. Place the finished paste in a ziplock bag, and place the bagged paste in a second bag and seal well. Allow the gum paste to mature for 24 hours before use, storing it in a cool environment. When ready to use the paste, cut off a small amount and knead a little vegetable shortening into the paste. If coloring at this stage, knead the color into the paste until the desired shade is achieved. When not in use, store the paste in the refrigerator. Always store the paste in ziplock bags. The paste will keep in the refrigerator for approximately 6 months.

Easy Gum Paste Recipe

- *1 pound (0.45 kg) rolled fondant*
- *1 tablespoon (15 g) Tylose powder*

Knead Tylose powder into the rolled fondant.

50/50 Paste

50/50 paste is a blend of rolled fondant and gum paste. This recipe is used for many accent techniques to give strength to the rolled fondant while still being soft enough to eat when biting into the cookie. It should not be used as a covering for the cookies.

50/50 Paste

- *1 part gum paste*
- *1 part rolled fondant*

Knead and soften the gum paste. Knead and soften the rolled fondant. Work the gum paste and fondant together until they are thoroughly blended.

Edible Glue

This recipe makes an edible glue for attaching gum paste and rolled fondant pieces to the cookies. Note: If the pieces to be glued are both soft, you can substitute egg whites for edible glue. A small amount of glue is all that is needed. Since the glue dries with a shine, be careful not to use too much or the glue will seep and be visible. Tylose is a manufactured gum. Be sure to use food-grade Tylose.

- *1 tablespoon (15 g) Tylose powder*
- *1½ cups (360 mL) water*

Boil water. Whisk in the Tylose powder and stir until dissolved. Store in the refrigerator until ready for use.

Piping Gel

Piping gel, available commercially, is a clear, flavorless material that works well for an edible glue. Use piping gel sparingly or the gel will seep and be visible.

CLAY EXTRUDERS

You can use a clay extruder to create a variety of lines, textures, and details with consistent thickness. Extruder kits include an assortment of interchangeable disks.

1 Knead and soften rolled fondant or gum paste. Roll a cylinder of paste the length of the extruder and slightly smaller in diameter than the extruder barrel.

2 Feed the barrel of the extruder from the bottom.

3 Choose the desired disk and attach to the extruder.

4 Twist the handle on the gun to release the paste.

5 Use a paring knife or a spatula with a thin blade to cut extruded paste. Attach to the cookie using piping gel.

1

3

2

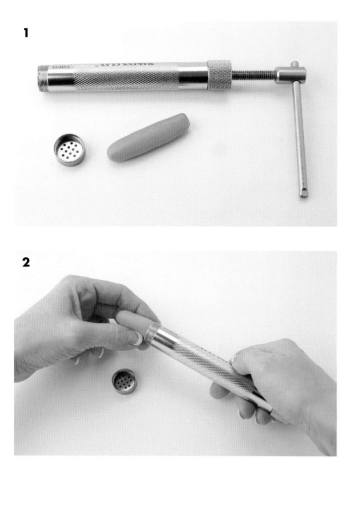

4

5

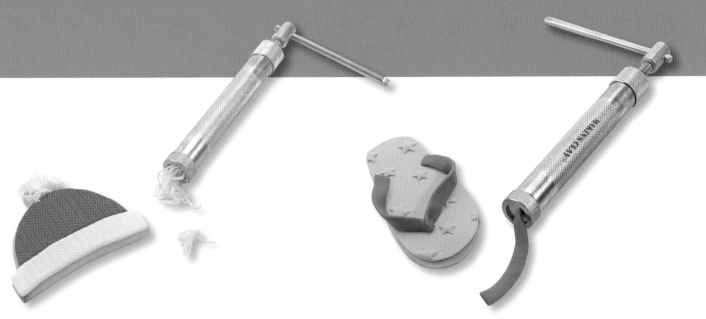

Multiple round openings are used for hair, straw, and fur.

Flat disks are used for ribbons or flat bands.

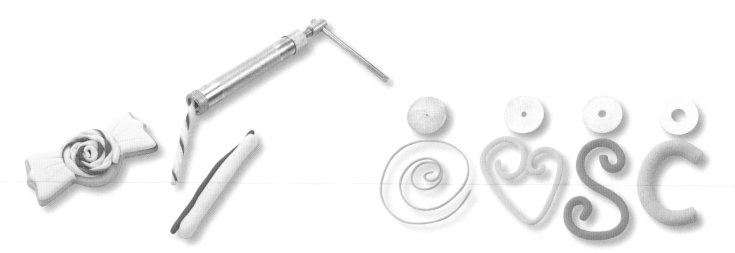

The clovers and hexagons are used for making ropes. Clovers create the most striking twist design. When the fondant is released from the extruder, twist for the rope effect. Combine colors for a multicolored rope.

Most sets contain numerous disks for making various designs. Single round openings are used for vines, stems, letters, and borders.

Extruder Tip

If you are struggling to release the paste from the extruder, try warming the paste. First, remove the paste from the extruder. Then place the paste cylinder in the microwave for 2 or 3 seconds, or until just warm. Put the paste back into the extruder and try again. Be careful that the fondant doesn't get too warm, or details may be lost.

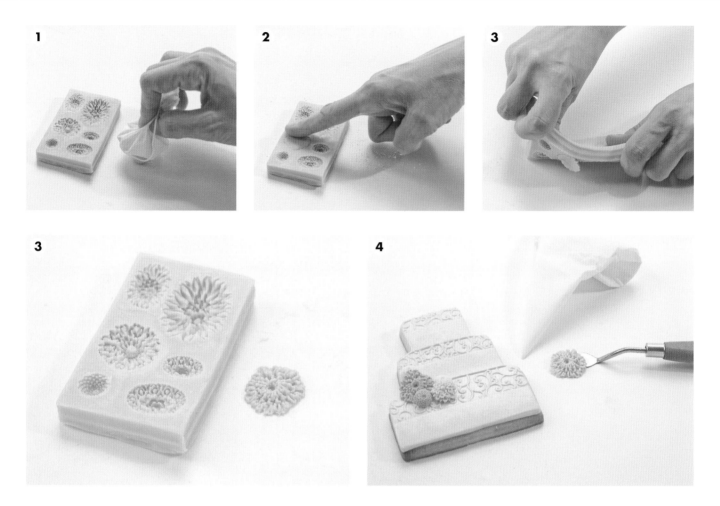

MOLDING WITH SILICONE

Silicone molds are available in several styles and give fantastic detail for accent pieces on cookies. Be sure the silicone mold is washed and dried thoroughly before using, as silicone easily picks up specks of dust.

1 Knead and soften the rolled fondant. Form into a ball. Dust the ball with cornstarch.

2 Press the ball into the mold, filling the entire cavity. Scrape off excess with a thin palette knife. Press against the edges of the cavity with your fingers to ensure the edges are clean.

3 Hold the silicone mold with both hands and press in the center with your thumbs to release the rolled fondant.

4 Attach the molded piece to the cookie using piping gel or edible glue.

Clinging

If the silicone mold is deep or highly detailed, the rolled fondant may be difficult to remove. If this happens, place the filled mold in the freezer for about 15 minutes to allow the fondant to set firm before releasing.

MOLDING WITH CANDY MOLDS

Candy molds are an affordable alternative to silicone molds. Take note, however, that the molds are not flexible like silicone and so it may be more difficult to remove the rolled fondant piece from the mold.

1 Knead and soften the rolled fondant. Form into a ball. Dust the ball with cornstarch.

2 Press ball into the mold, filling the entire cavity. Scrape off excess with a thin palette knife. Use your index finger to smooth edges of the fondant.

3 Use a bit of excess fondant to pull the sides from the mold. When the sides are pulled away, use the excess paste to remove the molded accent.

Letting Go

If the rolled fondant or gum paste is not releasing, spray the candy molds with a grease cooking spray. Remove excess grease with a paper towel. Although spraying the candy molds with a cooking spray may make the pieces easier to release, some details may be lost.

4 Attach the molded piece to the cookie using edible glue or piping gel.

USING A PASTA MACHINE

A pasta machine is used to efficiently and evenly roll sheets of rolled fondant or gum paste. Self-standing pasta machines are available as well as pasta attachments for popular stand mixers. The subsequent chapters discuss cutting rolled fondant that has been rolled thin. The pasta machine is ideal when rolling out rolled fondant for accents on cookies.

1 Roll the rolled fondant approximately ¼" (6 mm) thick. Cut the rolled fondant slightly smaller than the width of the pasta machine roller. Set the pasta machine to the widest setting (usually setting 1). Place the rolled fondant in the pasta machine. Crank the handle or turn on the mixer if an attachment is used and roll the rolled fondant through the machine. Take hold of the rolled fondant as it is fed through the machine. If the rolled fondant bunches or wrinkles, the rolled fondant was too thick when fed through the roller. Roll the rolled fondant thinner and try again.

2 Move to the next thinner setting and feed the paste again.

3 Continue feeding the paste, moving to a thinner setting with each roll.

1

2

3

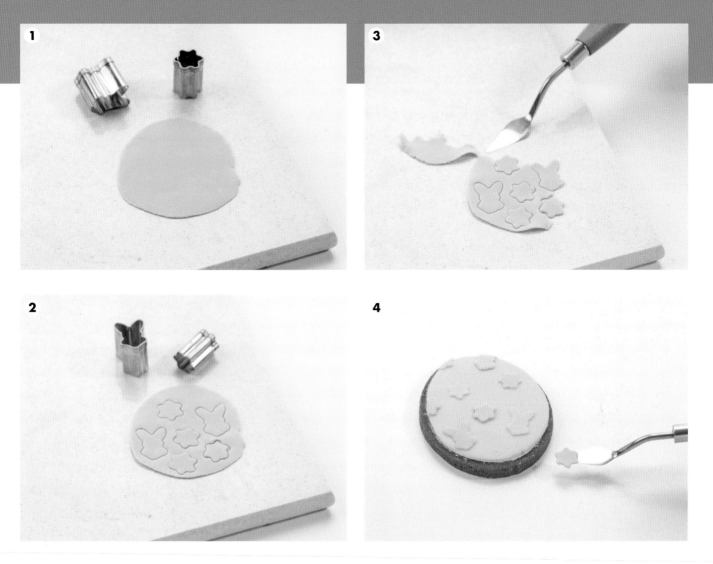

GUM PASTE AND MINI-COOKIE CUTTERS

Choose from dozens of mini-cookie cutters to accent cookies. Gum paste cutters used for cake decorating provide additional design options. Follow these instructions for basic rolling and cutting using mini-cookie cutters or most gum paste cutters. When cutting accents, the thinner the rolled fondant, the daintier and more professional the cutout piece will appear. Before starting, be sure the countertop is free of any debris or small particles. For the sharpest cut, the cutter's edge needs to be clean and free of crusted rolled fondant. Wipe the cutter with a damp cloth to remove crusted fondant.

General Directions

1 Knead and soften the rolled fondant. Dust the countertop surface with cornstarch. Roll the rolled fondant thin (#4 on a pasta machine [0.6 mm]). You can also use the smallest size (2 mm) of perfection strips instead of a pasta machine, but the cut piece will not be as dainty. Rub the surface of a plastic placemat with a thin layer of solid vegetable shortening. Place rolled fondant on the plastic placemat. Rub a thin layer of solid vegetable shortening on the cutting side of the cutter. The shortening should not be visible on the board or cutter.

2 Cut out shapes with the desired cutter.

3 Pull away excess rolled fondant with a small palette knife.

4 Slide a long spatula with a thin blade under the cut piece, and lift gently. If the piece is stretching when lifting, allow it to set for a few minutes before lifting. Attach the piece to the iced cookie using piping gel or edible glue, page 104.

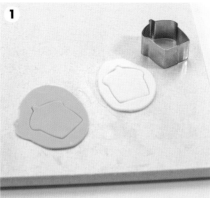

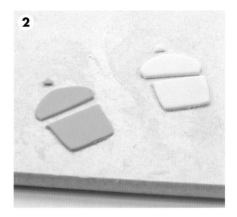

Coloring White Cut Shapes

Add details to white cut rolled fondant shapes with food color markers. Allow the rolled fondant to crust several hours before coloring.

Pieced-Together Designs

Shapes can be cut into sections and replaced with contrasting colors.

1. Knead and soften the rolled fondant. Dust the countertop surface with cornstarch. Roll at least two colors of rolled fondant thin (#4 on a pasta machine [0.6 mm]). You can also use the smallest size (2 mm) of perfection strips instead of a pasta machine, but the cut piece will not be as dainty. Rub the

surface of a plastic placemat with a thin layer of solid vegetable shortening. Place the two pieces of rolled fondant on the plastic placemat. Rub a thin layer of solid vegetable shortening on the cutting side of the cutter. The shortening should not be visible on the board or cutter. Cut out shapes in both colors with desired cutter.

2. Pull away excess rolled fondant with a small palette knife. Cut the shapes into sections.

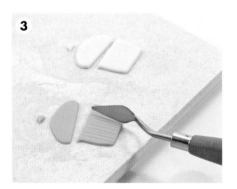

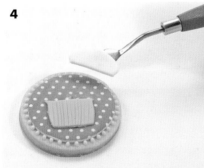

3. Texture if desired.

4. Slide a long spatula with a thin blade under the cut piece, and lift gently. If the piece is stretching when lifting, allow it to set for a

few minutes before lifting. Arrange the shape on the cookie, and piece contrasting colors together. Attach with piping gel.

1

Cutters with Embossed Details

Some cutters have embossed details. Be sure the cutter has a thin layer of shortening on all the cutting areas of the cutter.

1 Knead and soften the rolled fondant. Dust the countertop surface with cornstarch. Roll the rolled fondant thin (#4 on a pasta machine [0.6 mm]). You can also use the smallest size (2 mm) of perfection strips instead of a pasta machine, but the cut piece will not be as dainty. Rub the surface of a plastic placemat with a thin layer of solid vegetable shortening. Place the rolled fondant on the plastic placemat. Rub a thin layer of solid vegetable shortening on the cutting side of the cutter. The shortening should not be visible on the board or cutter. Cut out shapes with desired cutter.

2 Pull away excess rolled fondant with a small palette knife.

3 Slide a long spatula with a thin blade under the cut piece. Lift the piece gently. If the piece is stretching when lifting, allow it to set for a few minutes before lifting.

4 Attach the piece to the iced cookie using piping gel or edible glue, page 104.

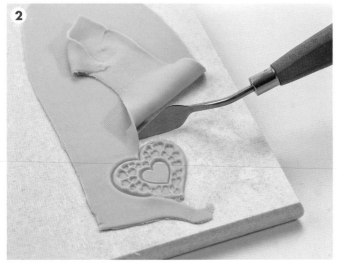

2

3

4

PATCHWORK CUTTERS

Patchwork cutters are a brand of cutters imported from the United Kingdom. The Patchwork cutters shown here are designed for appliqué style of decorating. The cutters can be used either to cut a single piece with an embossed design when gentle pressure is applied, or to cut the design into several pieces when firm pressure is applied. Gum paste is best suited for Patchwork cutters, but rolled fondant or 50/50 paste may also be used. The gum paste must be rolled thin, or else the cookie will be very hard when bitten. For the softest covered cookie, use rolled fondant; be aware, however, that Patchwork cutters are a little trickier to use with rolled fondant.

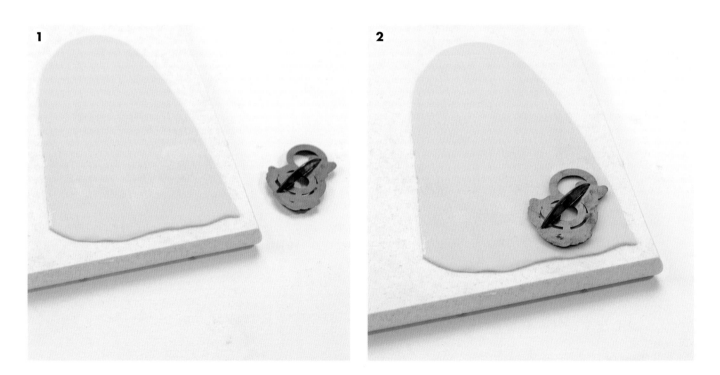

Patchwork Cutouts

1 Knead and soften the gum paste. Dust the work surface with cornstarch. Roll the paste thin (#5 on a pasta machine). Rub the surface of a plastic placemat with a thin layer of solid vegetable shortening. Rub a thin layer of solid vegetable shortening on the cutting side of the Patchwork cutter. The shortening should not be visible. Place the rolled gum paste on the plastic placemat.

2 Gently press all over the cutter to emboss the design. Press firmly around the edges to cut the outside edge of the gum paste piece.

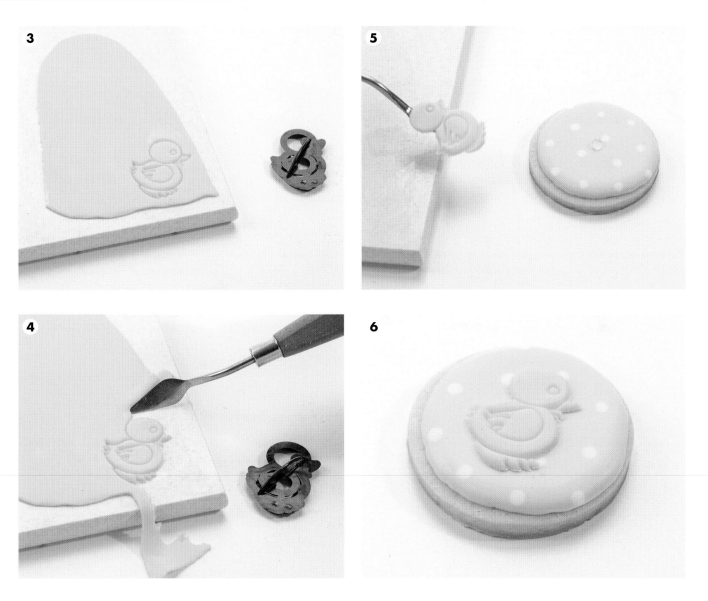

3 Remove the cutter.

4 Pull away excess gum paste using a palette knife.

5 Lift the cut piece using a spatula with a thin blade.

6 Attach to the cookie with a dot of piping gel.

Too Much Pressure

If pieces are coming apart while lifting, you may have applied too much pressure all over when cutting. Firm pressure should only be used around the outside edges if not creating an appliqué style. Gentle pressure should be used to emboss.

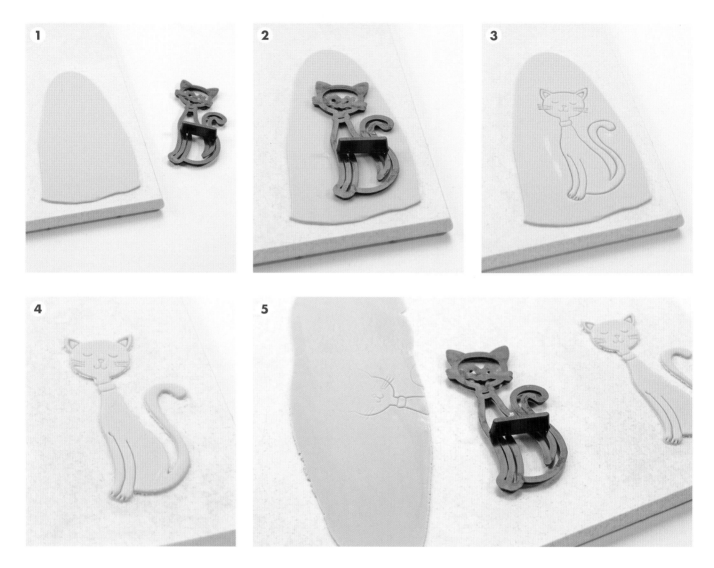

Patchwork Appliqué Style

1 Knead and soften the gum paste. Dust the work surface with cornstarch. Roll the gum paste thin (#5 on a pasta machine). Rub the surface of a plastic placemat with a thin layer of solid vegetable shortening. Rub a thin layer of solid vegetable shortening on the cutting side of the patchwork cutter. The shortening should not be visible.

2 Gently press all over the cutter to emboss the design, and press firmly around the edges to cut the outside edge of the gum paste piece.

3 Remove the cutter.

4 Pull away excess gum paste using a knife with a thin, small blade.

5 Repeat step 1 with a contrasting color of gum paste. Firmly press the cutter all over to cut the pieces apart. In this example, all that is needed is the cat's collar.

Tiny Pieces

Remove tiny pieces using a straight pin.

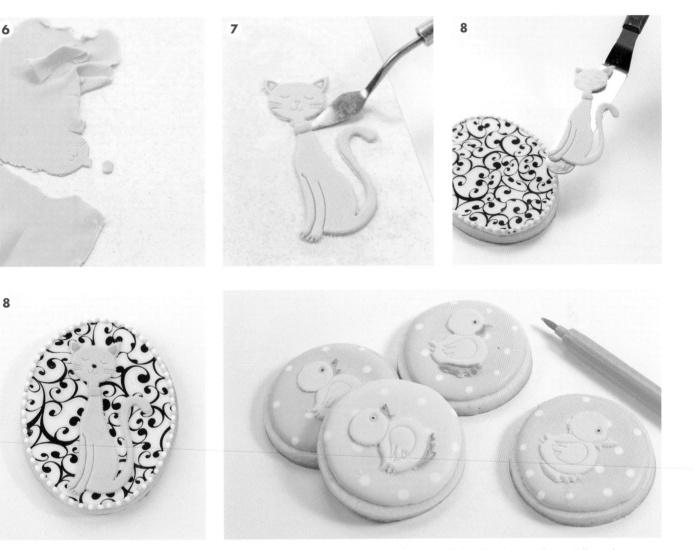

Patchwork-cut shapes can be colored with food color markers. Allow the piece to firm for several hours before coloring.

6 Remove excess gum paste using a palette knife.

7 Arrange the cut pieces on the first cut shape, layering the pieces.

8 Lift the piece and place on the cookie.

Mexican Paste

Each Patchwork cutter includes a recipe for Mexican Paste, which has similar properties to gum paste. Feel free to substitute gum paste for Mexican Paste.

BOWS

The following instructions are for a 2" (5.1 cm) wide bow, but the bow can be scaled to fit the cookie.

Hand-Cut Bows

1 Knead and soften the rolled fondant. Dust the work surface with cornstarch. Roll the rolled fondant thin (#5 on a pasta machine). Rub the surface of a plastic placemat with a thin layer of solid vegetable shortening. Place the rolled gum paste on the plastic placemat. Cut two ½" x 2" (1.3 x 5.1 cm) strips of rolled fondant.

2 Brush the ends of the strips with edible glue. Fold the strips in half and pinch the ends together to form pleats.

3 Put the folded loops together. Cut a ¼" x ½" (6 mm x 1.3 cm) strip for the knot.

4 Brush edible glue on the back of the knot strip. Attach the knot to the bow, pressing the ends under the loopy part of the bow.

5 For the bow streamers, cut two ½" x 2" (1.3 x 5.1 cm) strips of gum paste. Notch one end of each streamer using a paring knife. Pinch the other end.

6 Arrange the streamers on the cookie. Attach with piping gel.

7 Arrange loops on the cookie. Attach with piping gel.

Bows from a Cutter

1 Knead and soften the rolled fondant. Dust the countertop surface with cornstarch. Roll the rolled fondant thin (#4 on a pasta machine [0.6 mm]). You can also use the smallest size (2 mm) of perfection strips instead of a pasta machine, but the cut piece will not be as dainty. Rub the surface of a plastic placemat with a thin layer of solid vegetable shortening. Place the rolled fondant on the plastic placemat. Rub a thin layer of solid vegetable shortening on the cutting side of the bow cutter. The shortening should not be visible on the board or cutter.

2 Cut out the bow pieces with the bow cutter.

3 Pull away excess rolled fondant with a small palette knife.

4 Place the streamers on the cookie. Attach with piping gel.

5 Fold the sides of the bow loops.

6 Place the loops on the cookie. Attach with piping gel. Brush edible glue on the back of the knot strip. Attach the knot to the bow, pressing the ends under the loopy part of the bow.

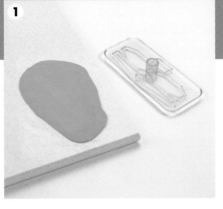

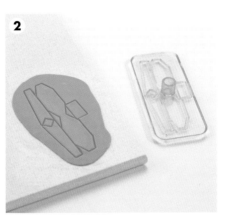

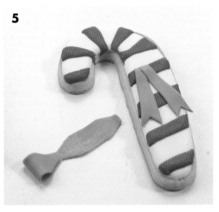

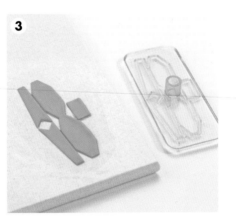

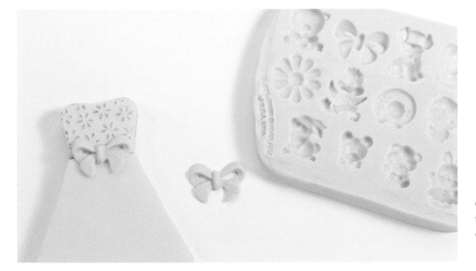

Candy molds and silicone molds are the quickest and easiest way to create a rolled fondant bow.

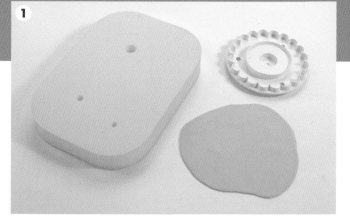

RUFFLES

Ruffles add a feminine touch to cookies. Make them with a simple cut strip of 50/50 paste, or use one of the several frill cutters available. The Garrett Frill Cutter is a frill cutter designed by cake decorator Elaine Garrett to create elegant ruffles with a natural curve; however, the ruffle design is limited. Straight frill cutters are available in several styles and ruffle widths. For best results, use the 50/50 paste recipe; you may also use rolled fondant.

1 Knead and soften the 50/50 paste. Dust the work surface with cornstarch. Roll the paste thin (#4 on a pasta machine [0.6 mm]).

2 Use the Garrett Frill cutter to cut the 50/50 paste. Remove the center circle.

3 Cut the ring open with a paring knife or a spatula with a thin blade.

4 Place the strip close to the edge on a Celpad. Use a Celpin and roll the Celpin back and forth to thin and frill the edge. The amount of pressure used will determine how frilly the ruffle.

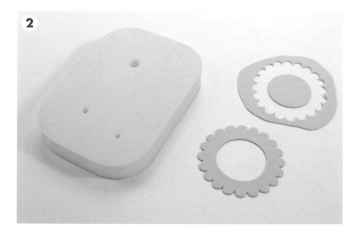

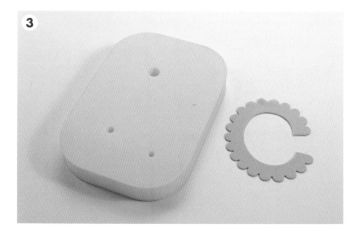

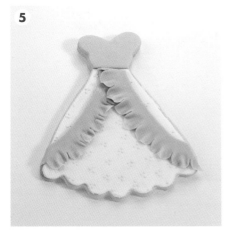

5

6

A ribbon cutter is another cutter that works well for a basic, straight ruffle. Using a straight cutter is the easiest way to master ruffling.

5 Pipe dots of piping gel on the cookie where the ruffle will be placed. Place the ruffle on the piping gel dots.

6 Additional swags may be added. Pipe a line of piping gel just above the top edge of the first ruffle. Then attach the second ruffle just above the first.

1

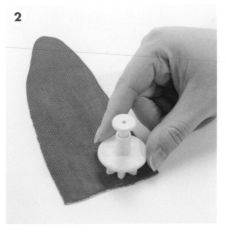

2

PLUNGER CUTTERS

Plunger cutters are gum-paste cutters that quickly cut flowers and other accents. The piece is cut, and then the plunger is pushed to release it. Many of the plungers have veining or details, which add extra charm to the cut piece. Roll the rolled fondant thin for delicate, dainty pieces.

Simple Plunger Cutters

1 Knead and soften the rolled fondant. Dust the work surface with cornstarch. Roll the rolled fondant thin (#4 on a pasta machine [0.6 mm]). Dust the surface of a plastic placemat with cornstarch. Place rolled fondant on the plastic placemat.

2 Hold the plunger by the base and cut the shape.

Lift the cutter. While the fondant is still in the cutter, run your thumb over the edges of the cutter to ensure a clean cut.

(continued)

3

3 Press the plunger to release shape.

4

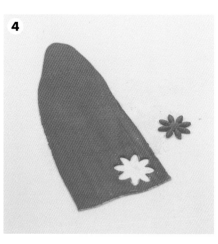

4 Attach the shape to the cookie with edible glue, or cup petals using the following directions.

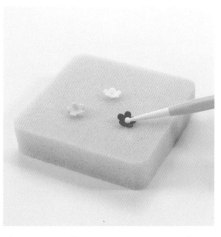

Place petite flowers on a piece of foam. Cup the petals with a ball tool.

Place larger flowers in a flower former to cup the petals. Allow to dry.

When the flowers are dry, attach to the cookies using piping gel.

Plunger cutters are available in many shapes. The shapes can be placed on the cookies immediately after cutting.

1

2

3

Plunger Cutters with Veining and Detailing

1 Knead and soften the rolled fondant. Dust the work surface with cornstarch. Roll the rolled fondant thin (#4 on a pasta machine [0.6 mm]). Dust the surface of a plastic placemat with cornstarch. Place the rolled fondant on the plastic placemat. Hold the plunger by the base and cut the shape. Do not use the plunger.

2 Lift the cutter. While the fondant is still in the cutter, run your thumb over the edges of the cutter to ensure a clean cut. Place the cutter back on the work surface. Press the plunger to emboss the veins.

3 Lift and press plunger to release the shape.

3

4

4 Attach shapes to the cookies with edible glue.

No Sticking

If the cut shapes are sticking to the table, run a spatula with a very thin blade underneath to lift the cut shape from the work surface.

Packaging Cookies

Once the cookies are decorated, they can be arranged on a plate or packaged for favors. The icing needs to be firm or hardened before the cookies can be placed into bags. Icings that are still soft or are not completely dry run the risk of the details being smashed or broken. Run sugar iced cookies should be ready for packaging after 24 hours. Rolled fondant and buttercream iced cookies will form a crust, but will still be delicate for packaging. Candy coated and egg wash glazed cookies are ready for packaging within an hour or two.

PACKAGING COOKIES IN CELLO BAGS

Individual cellophane bags are an affordable method of packaging while providing a clear view of the decorated cookie. A simple coordinating ribbon seals the bag. For individual cookies, a flat (not gusseted) cellophane bag provides the cleanest look. Be sure the seam of the bag is in the back. Although the bags are clear, the seam is visible.

Placing a header with an accent ribbon adds a touch of extra color. Fold a piece of cardstock in half. Attach the header using double-sided tape.

Cardstock in a cellophane bag provides a backdrop for the cookie to stand out. Choose a subtle print so that the background does not take away from the decorated cookie. The cookies should be placed in the bag just before giving, as the butters and grease from the cookie will soak into the cardstock soon after being placed in the bag, leaving unsightly grease spots.

A stack of cookies made using the same cutter are elegant when arranged in a cello bag. These cookies must have an icing that is durable, such as these eyelet rolled fondant–covered cookies.

OTHER PACKAGING

A candy box provides a safe covering for these Christmas trees and wreaths piped with buttercream. Candy boxes should be made of food-grade materials. Use food-safe tissue paper to line boxes and tins that are not made of food-grade material.

Cookie tins are a classic container for gift giving. Be sure the tin is food safe, or line the tin with food safe tissue paper or parchment paper.

Choosing a container first can inspire the decorating. The design for these cookies was planned to coordinate with the container.

A clear cookie jar showcases cookies. Cookies must be durable, or details will be smashed or broken.

PACKAGING COOKIES FOR SHIPPING

If the recipient of the decorated cookies lives far away, the cookies can be shipped. When baking cookies to ship, choose simple shapes. Shapes with thin areas may break (for example, long, thin antlers on a reindeer are likely to arrive with the antlers broken off). Some cookie icings are better suited for shipped cookies than others. Chocolate-coated cookies dry completely firm and are great for stacking. However, in warm weather, the chocolate may melt and create a mess for the recipient. Run sugar–iced cookies and egg wash–glazed cookies are both excellent choices. See the chart on page 47 for more information on cookies that ship well. Pack the cookies in a container with a tight seal, such as cookie tins or food storage containers. Containers with a tight seal are the best choice to keep the cookies fresh as well as for keeping out critters. Cookies that sit in shipping warehouses have a greater chance for unwelcome visitors, such as ants, to invade the package. Select next-, second-, or third-day services to decrease the chance of infestation.

1 Place a layer of cookies in a container or tin. The cookies should be packed tightly together without the cookies overlapping. Place crumpled parchment paper to keep the first layer of cookies from jostling and breaking. The crumpled paper should be about the same depth of the cookies. Shake the container gently to ensure cookies are not shifting.

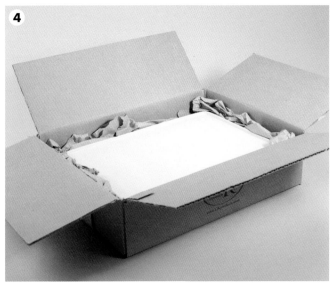

2 Repeat step 1 with a second layer. Add more layers if desired.

3 Place a sheet of parchment paper on top of the final layer of cookies. Place crumpled sheets of parchment on top if there is still space.

4 Place the lid on the container. Gently jostle the container. You should not hear or feel any cookies shifting. Add a layer of crumpled newspaper or packing material in the bottom of a sturdy cardboard box. Place the container or tin in the box, and surround it with tightly wadded newspaper or packing material to prevent shifting.

5 Add another layer of wadded packing material on top of the container. Tightly seal the box with shipping tape. Writing "Fragile" on the box or using tape printed with "Fragile" alerts the shipping provider that the items inside the box are easily broken.

Cookie Bouquets

A cookie bouquet showcases decorated cookies in a container, creating a lovely presentation that is also delicious to eat! Individual cookies can be placed in a small vase to give as a party favor, or several cookies may be arranged in a larger container for a terrific gift or centerpiece. It is important to properly bake the cookies on a stick, following directions on page 22. Be sure the cookies are not too loose or they may fall off the stick. Loose cookies can be secured by adding a bit of royal icing on the back. Allow the royal icing to harden before arranging. The sticks are arranged in the container and held in place by Styrofoam or candy clay. It is easier to rearrange sticks in candy clay than in Styrofoam. Holes poked into Styrofoam are permanent, whereas candy clay can be pushed together to seal the holes. Candy clay adds additional weight to the container. If using Styrofoam, choose the fine-particle type and not Styrofoam made with tiny beads (about 2 mm). This type of Styrofoam breaks larger holes than desired, causing the cookie sticks to wobble.

SELECTING A CONTAINER

Choose a container that will complement the decorated cookies. I often select a container or vase before decorating and let the container inspire the color and design of the decorated cookies.

Flowerpots are sold in nearly all craft stores and work well as general containers for cookies.

Candy in a glass jar provides a color-ful vessel for cookies. Place a cylinder of candy clay in the center of the glass

jar. Leave enough space between the candy clay and the walls of the jar to allow the candy to fit. Add candy

around the cylinder of candy clay. Arrange the cookies. Add more candy to cover up the candy clay cylinder.

Gift bags are an inexpensive holder for cookie bouquets. However, since they are so lightweight, be sure to use candy clay instead of Styrofoam when arranging the cookies.

Almost any hollow container will work for holding the cookies on a stick. Shown is a cookie arrangement displayed in a small crate that resembles a garden fence.

CANDY CLAY

Candy clay is a simple combination of melted chocolate and corn syrup. The two combined ingredients make an edible clay that is similar in taste and texture to a Tootsie Roll. Candy clay is an ideal filler for the bouquets. It adds weight—and provides an additional treat for the recipient. One pound (0.45 kg) of candy clay will fill approximately two or three 5" (12.7 cm) containers, or six or seven 3" (7.6 cm) containers. One disadvantage is that once the candy clay is formed into the pot, it will become hard and may be difficult to remove. The recipient may need to spoon the mixture a little at a time to remove the clay. Another disadvantage of using candy clay is that it will melt if the bouquet is stored in a warm area or in direct sunlight. Treat the candy clay as you would a chocolate candy bar. If the container holding the candy clay is not food grade, line the container with plastic wrap before adding the candy clay.

Candy Clay

- *1 pound (0.45 kg) candy coating or chocolate*
- *⅔ cup (160 mL) of corn syrup*

Lay out a long sheet (approximately 24" [61 cm] long) of plastic wrap on the work surface. Melt the candy coating or chocolate. Stir in corn syrup. The mixture will immediately begin to thicken. Stir until the corn syrup is thoroughly mixed. Pour the thickened mixture onto the center of the plastic wrap. Tightly wrap the mixture. Allow the candy clay to set for several hours to become firm. After the candy clay becomes firm, knead to soften again before placing the candy clay in the container.

ARRANGING THE COOKIES

Once the cookies have been baked on a stick and are decorated, it's time to arrange them. Follow the instructions on page 22 for baking cookies with a stick. Begin with cookie sticks that are all the same length and then clip some for variety while making the arrangement. Generally, an odd number of cookies looks better than an even number in an arrangement; however, as long as the cookies are arranged with a variety of lengths, an even number will likely look fine.

1 Bake the cookies on a stick following instructions on page 22. Decorate as desired. If the container is not food safe, line the cookie container with plastic wrap. Fill the container approximately three-fourths full with candy clay, or cut Styrofoam to fit the container. Trim the plastic wrap so there is just enough plastic wrap to seal the Styrofoam or candy clay.

2 Insert the tallest cookie into the bouquet first. Hold onto the stick while inserting it near the back of the container filled with candy clay or Styrofoam. Do not hold onto the cookie or the cookie and its decorations may break or become damaged from the pressure.

3 Add the remaining cookies. Use shorter and shorter sticks as you place the cookies toward the front.

4 Cover the candy clay or Styrofoam with the plastic wrap that was used in the lining. Add coordinating candy to conceal the candy clay or Styrofoam.

Gallery

If you would like materials lists and complete directions for making any of these cookies, please visit http://www.creativepub.com/pages/cookiedecorating or www.cookiedecorating.com

Elephant and Bodysuit Cookies: Rolled Fondant, page 100; and Edible Frosting Sheets, page 146

Duck Bouquet: Buttercream Icing, page 82; and Cookie Bouquets, page 176

Teddy Bear Cookies: Run Sugar, page 64; and Flocking, page 138

Pink and White Wedding Cookies: Rolled Fondant, page 100; Detailed Piping with Royal Icing, page 74; and Accenting Cookies with Rolled Fondant, page 152

Brush-embroidered Wedding Cookies: Run Sugar, page 64; Detailed Piping with Royal Icing, page 74; and Brush Embroidery, page 142

Butterfly Cookie Bouquet: Rolled Fondant, page 100; Detailed Piping with Royal Icing, page 74; and Cookie Bouquets, page 176

Round Eyelet Cookies: Rolled Fondant, page 100; Eyelet Decorating, page 136; and Detailed Piping with Royal Icing, page 74

Brush-Embroidered Pink Flower Cookies: Run Sugar, page 64; Detailed Piping with Royal Icing, page 74; and Brush Embroidery, page 142

Princess Cookies: Run Sugar, page 64; and Shimmery, Sparkly Cookies, page 130

Chocolate-Coated Flower Cookies: Chocolate-Coated Cookies, page 114; and Accenting Cookies with Rolled Fondant, page 152

Beach Cookies: Rolled Fondant, page 100; Detailed Piping with Royal Icing, page 74; and Accenting Cookies with Rolled Fondant, page 152

Cupcake Cookies: Rolled Fondant, page 100; Detailed Piping with Royal Icing, page 74; and Accenting Cookies with Rolled Fondant, page 152

Brush-Embroidered Flower Cookies: Rolled Fondant, page 100; Detailed Piping with Royal Icing, page 74; and Brush Embroidery, page 142

Farm Animals: Cookie Cutter Shapes, page 23; Run Sugar, page 64; and Royal Icing, page 60

Flower Bouquets: Painted Cookies, page 78; and Cookie Bouquets, page 176

Retro Flower Cookies: Buttercream Icing, page 82; Edible Frosting Sheets, page 146; and Detailed Piping with Royal Icing, page 74

Birds in a Cage: Rolled Fondant, page 100; Edible Frosting Sheets, page 146; and Cookie Bouquets, page 176

Flocked Roses and Leaves: Run Sugar, page 64; and Flocking, page 138

Wild Valentine Cookies: Rolled Fondant, page 100; Detailed Piping with Royal Icing, page 74; Edible Frosting Sheets, page 146; and Accenting Cookies with Rolled Fondant, page 152

Bunny Cookies: Rolled Fondant, page 100; and Edible Frosting Sheets, page 146

Decorated Egg Cookies: Rolled Fondant, page 100; Detailed Piping with Royal Icing, page 74; Brush Embroidery, page 142; and Accenting Cookies with Rolled Fondant, page 152

Fall Leaves Cookies: Run Sugar, page 64; and Detailed Piping with Royal Icing, page 74

Stenciled Halloween Cookies: Run Sugar, page 64; Rolled Fondant, page 100; and Stencils, page 144

Sparkly Halloween Cookies: Run Sugar, page 64; Shimmery, Sparkly Cookies, page 130; and Detailed Piping with Royal Icing, page 74

Wintertime Cookies: Rolled Fondant, page 100; and Accenting Cookies with Rolled Fondant, page 152

Brush-Embroidered Winter Trees: Run Sugar, page 64; Brush Embroidery, page 142; and Accenting Cookies with Rolled Fondant, page 152

Christmas Face Cookies: Rolled Fondant, page 100; and Accenting Cookies with Rolled Fondant, page 152

Chocolate-Coated Christmas Trees and Presents: Chocolate-Coated Cookies, page 114; and Shimmery, Sparkly Cookies, page 130

Christmas Candy: Rolled Fondant, page 100; Accenting Cookies with Rolled Fondant, page 152; and Flocking, page 138

Christmas Cupcake Cookies: Buttercream Icing, page 82; and Edible Frosting Sheets, page 146

Round Eyelet Cookies: Rolled Fondant, page 100; Eyelet Decorating, page 136; and Detailed Piping with Royal Icing, page 74

Resources

The supplies used in this book may be found at your local cake and candy supply store or from Country Kitchen SweetArt, 4621 Speedway Drive, Fort Wayne, Indiana 46845, 260-482-4835, www.shopcountrykitchen.com. Manufacturers of specific items are listed below.

Americolor
food color
www.americolorcorp.com

Autumn Carpenter
texture sheets, jewel molds, stencils
www.autumncarpenter.com

Country Kitchen
complete baking and decorating store
www.shopcountrykitchen.com

FMM Sugarcraft
gum paste and fondant cutters
www.fmmsugarcraft.com

House on the Hill
wooden cookie molds
www.houseonthehill.net

JEM Cutters
gum paste and fondant cutters, flower formers
www.jemcutters.com

Patchwork Cutters
gum paste and fondant cutters
www.patchworkcutters.com

PME Arts and Crafts
gum paste and fondant cutters
www.pmeartsandcrafts.com

About the Author

Autumn Carpenter's passion for decorating started at a very young age. As a child, Autumn would spend time at the home of her grandmother, Hall of Fame sugar artist Mildred Brand. Later, her mother, Vi Whittington, became the owner of a retail cake and candy supply shop. Her grandmother provided many recipes, while her mother instilled a work ethic, a passion for the art, and served as the best teacher and mentor that Autumn has ever had.

Autumn Carpenter has demonstrated throughout the country. She has also served as a judge in cake decorating competitions. She has been a member, teacher, and demonstrator at the International Cake Exploration Society (ICES) for nearly 20 years.

Autumn is co-owner of Country Kitchen SweetArt, a retail cake and candy supply store. Country Kitchen SweetArt has been owned and operated within Autumn's family for over 45 years. The business caters to walk-in store sales, catalog sales, and an online store, www.shopcountrykitchen.com.

Autumn has developed her own line of useful tools and equipment for cake decorating and cookie decorating. Her cakes and products have been featured in numerous publications and magazines including *American Cake Decorating* and *Cake Central.* Her products can be found online as well as in many cake and candy supply stores throughout the United States and in several other countries. She is also the author of *The Complete Photo Guide to Cake Decorating.* Autumn's websites include www.autumncarpenter.com and www.cookiedecorating.com.

Acknowledgments

Thank you to my editor, Linda Neubauer, and the rest of the CPi staff for giving me an opportunity to write a second book.

Thanks to Dan Brand for photographing all of the finished projects. He takes amazing photographs. A special thanks to my mom, Vi Whittington, for her giving personality and willingness to assist wherever I needed.

Most of all, thank you to my family for their patience with me throughout this seemingly never-ending process.

Index